This Coloring Book Belongs To:

Illustrated By Adam Meeks
instagram.com/impurvisions

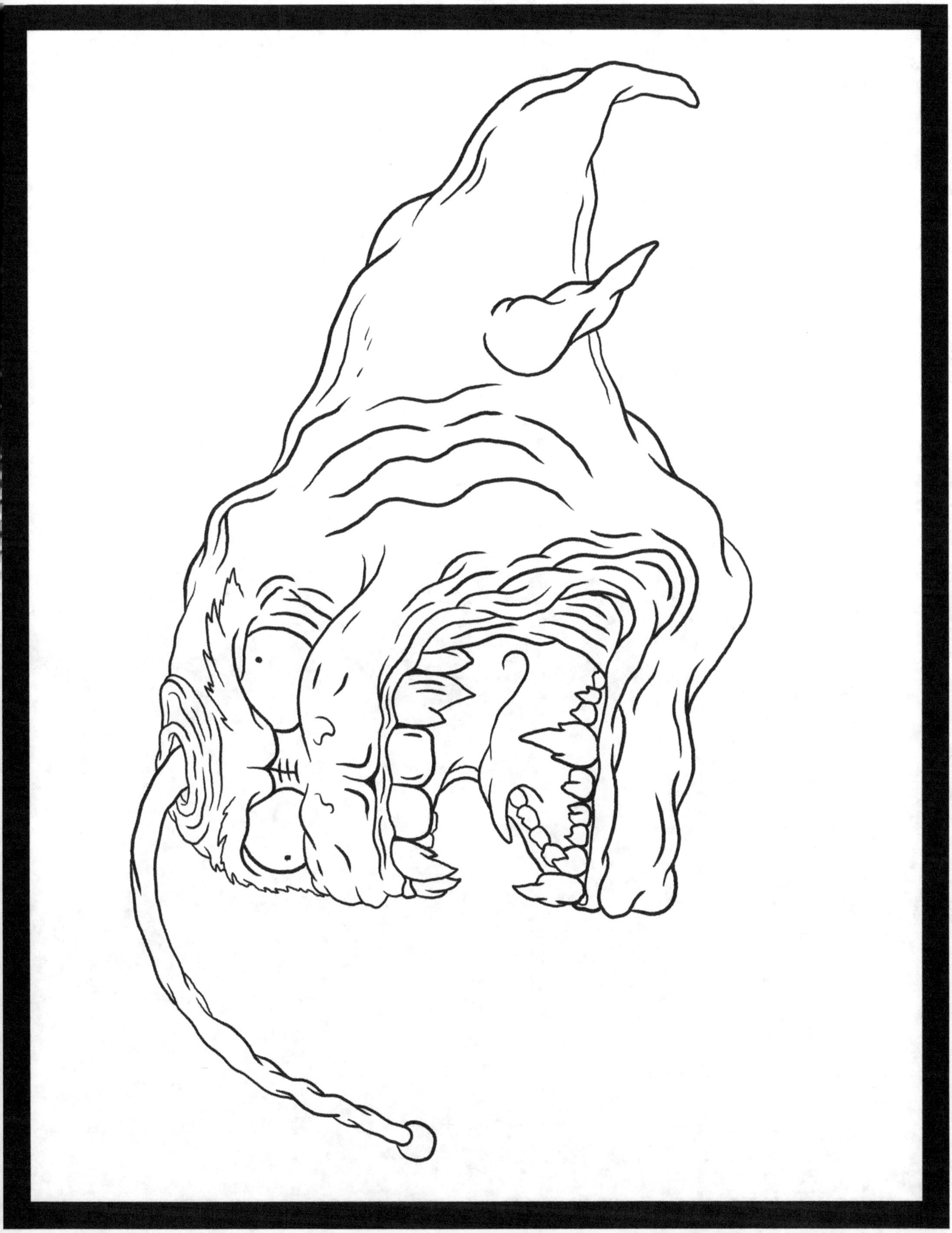

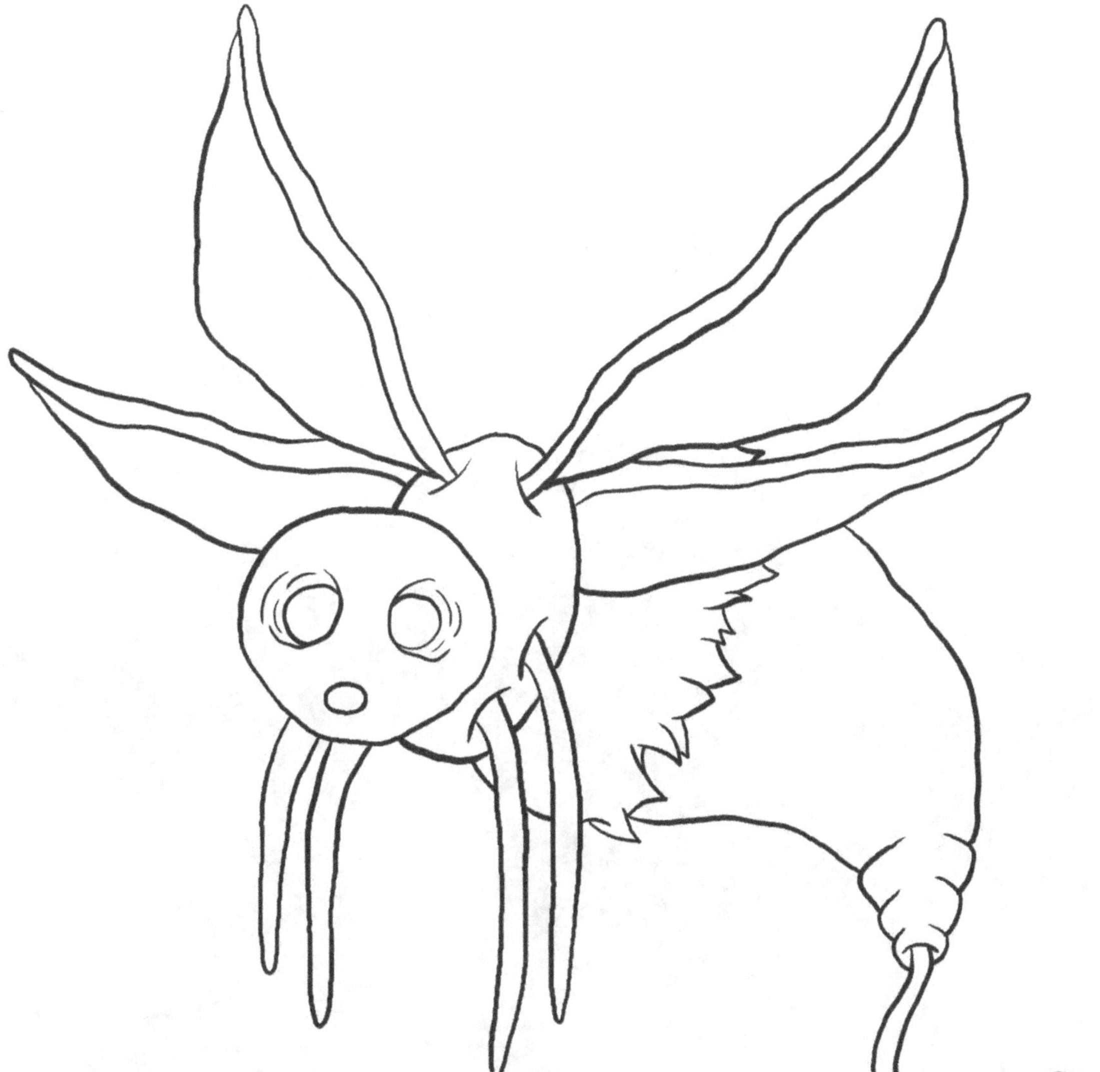

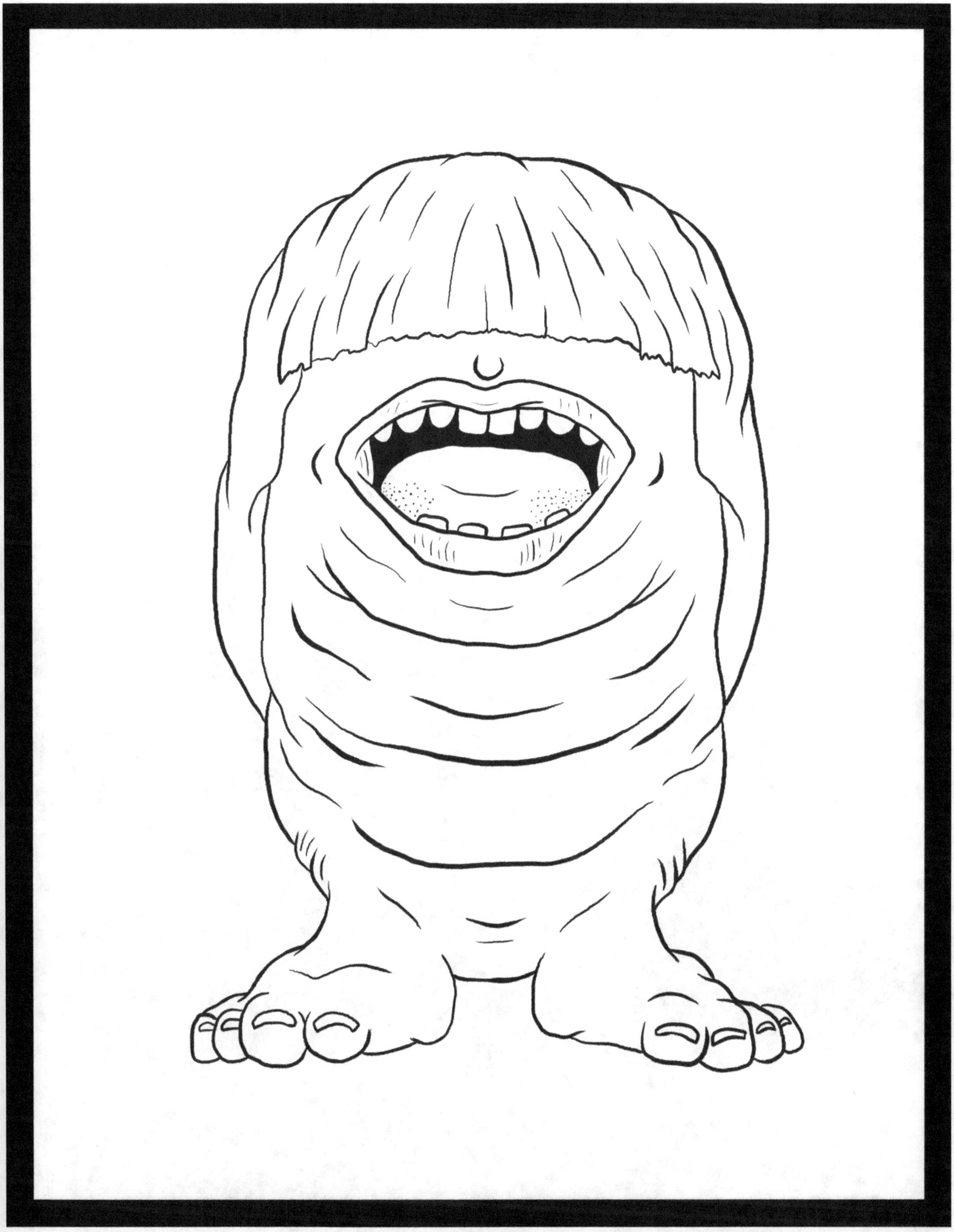

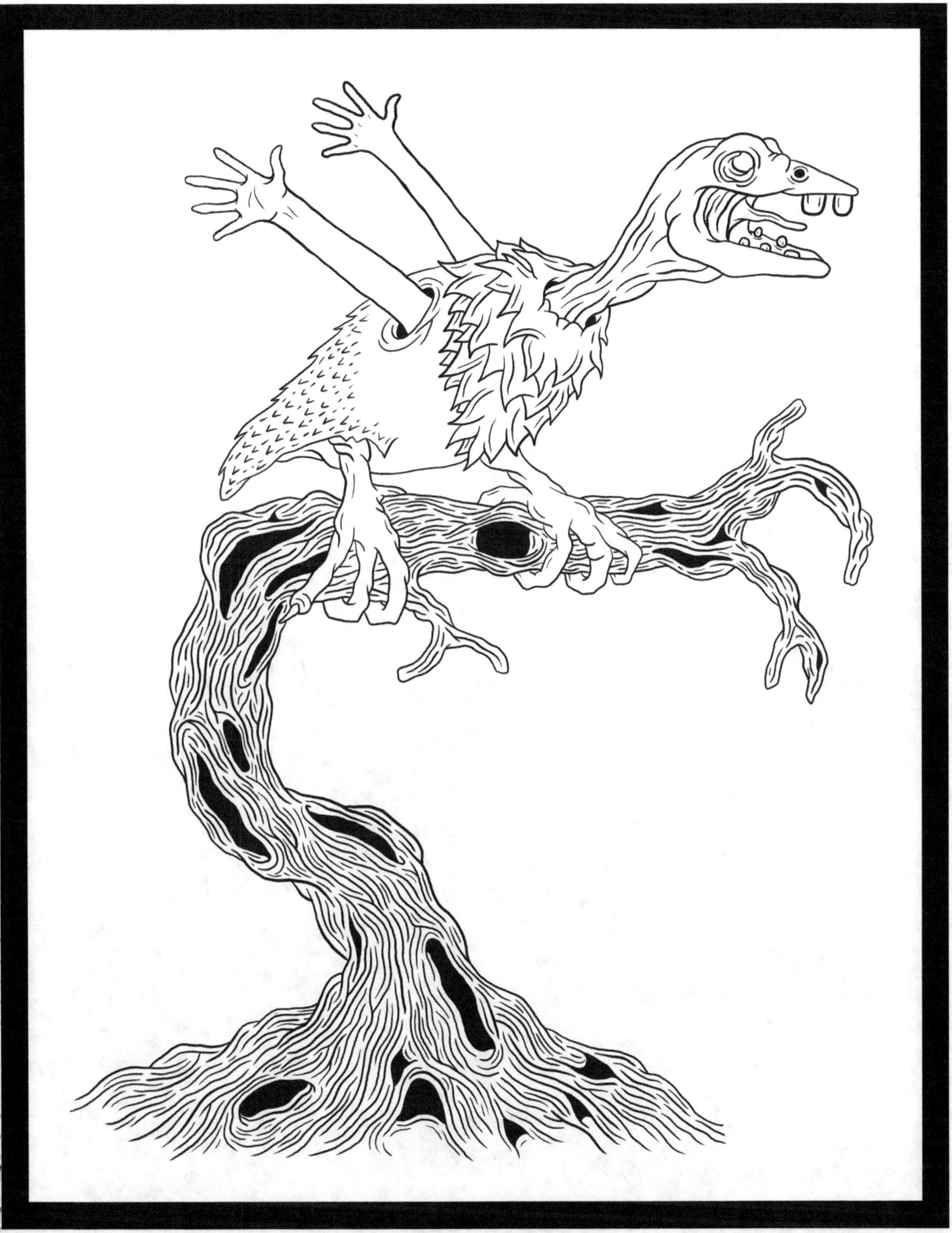

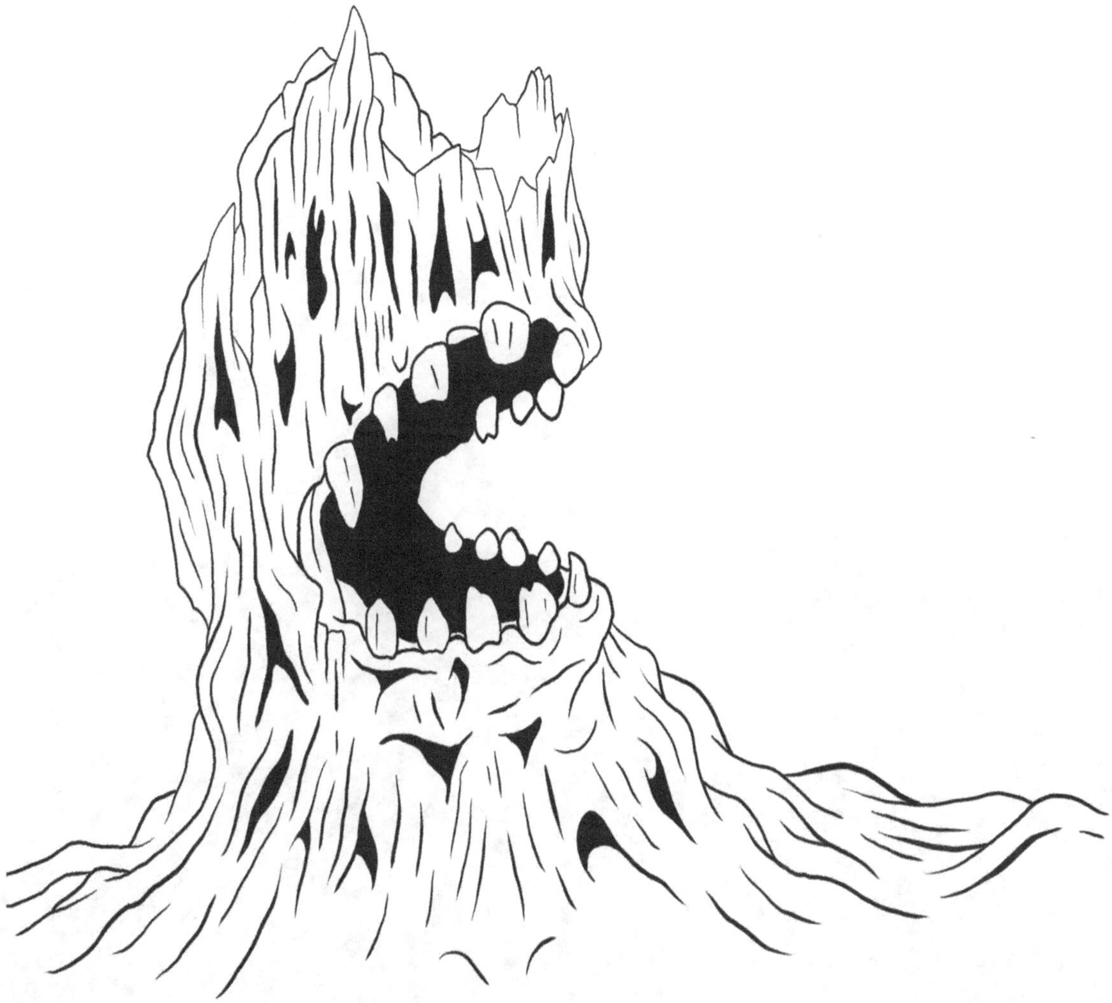

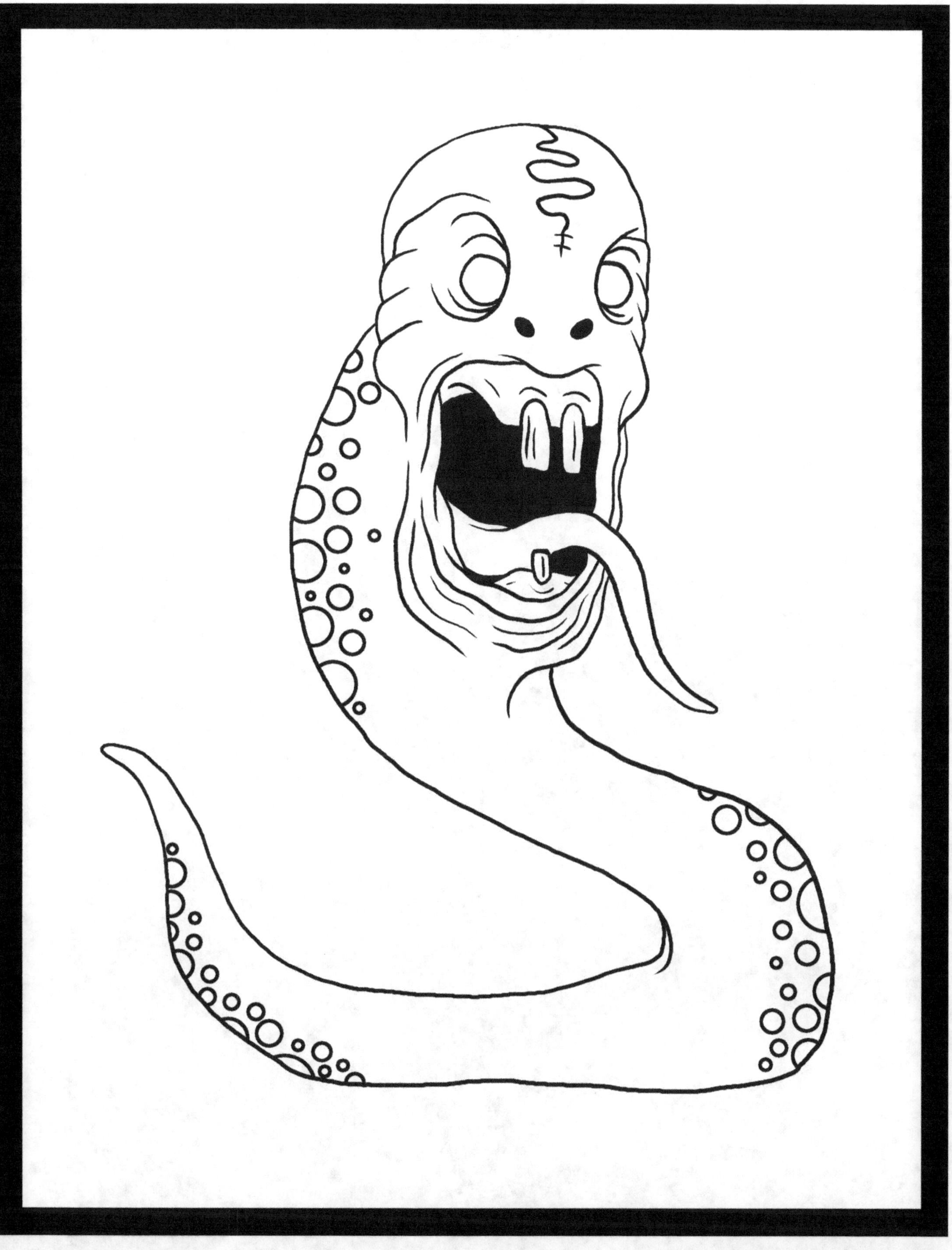

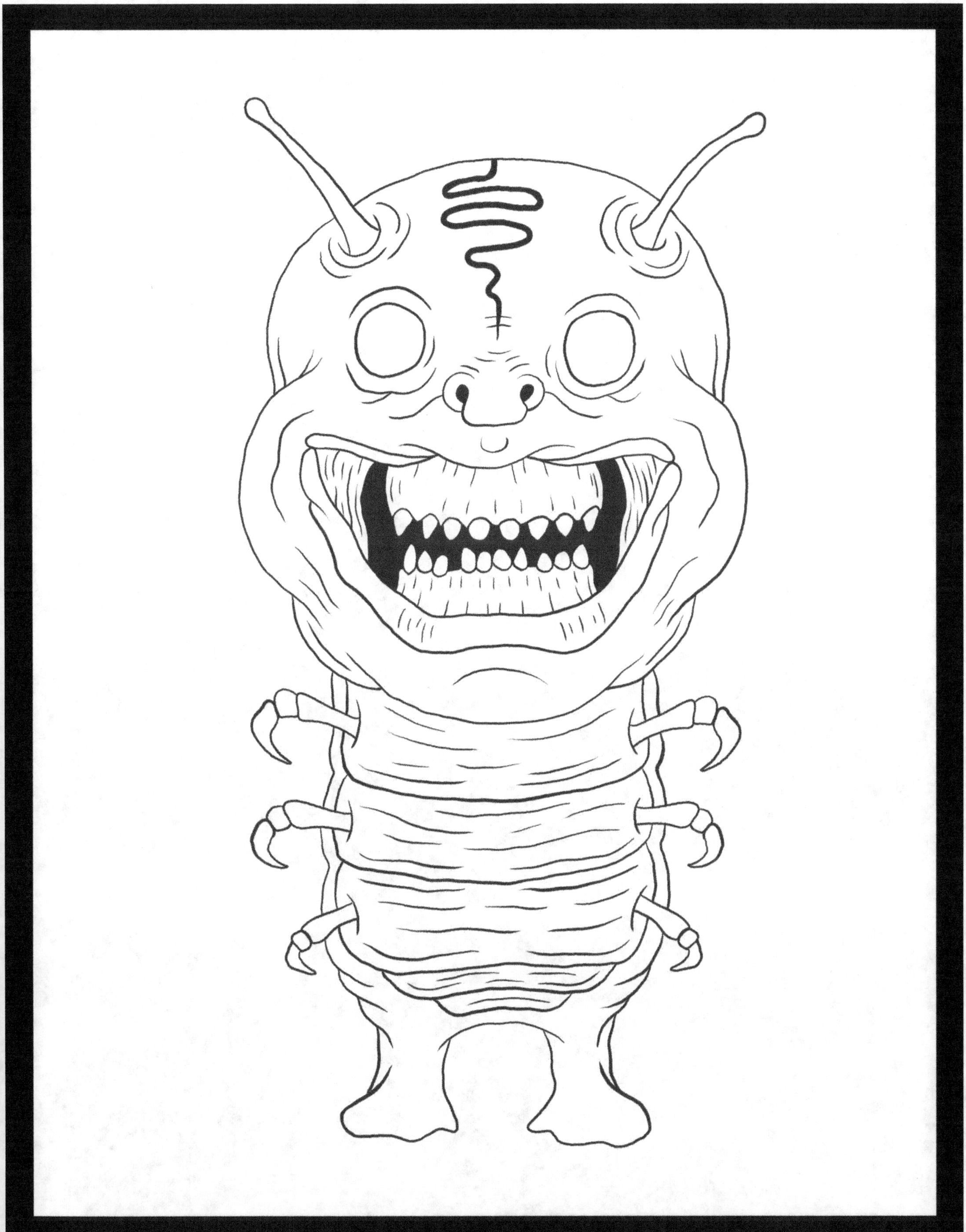

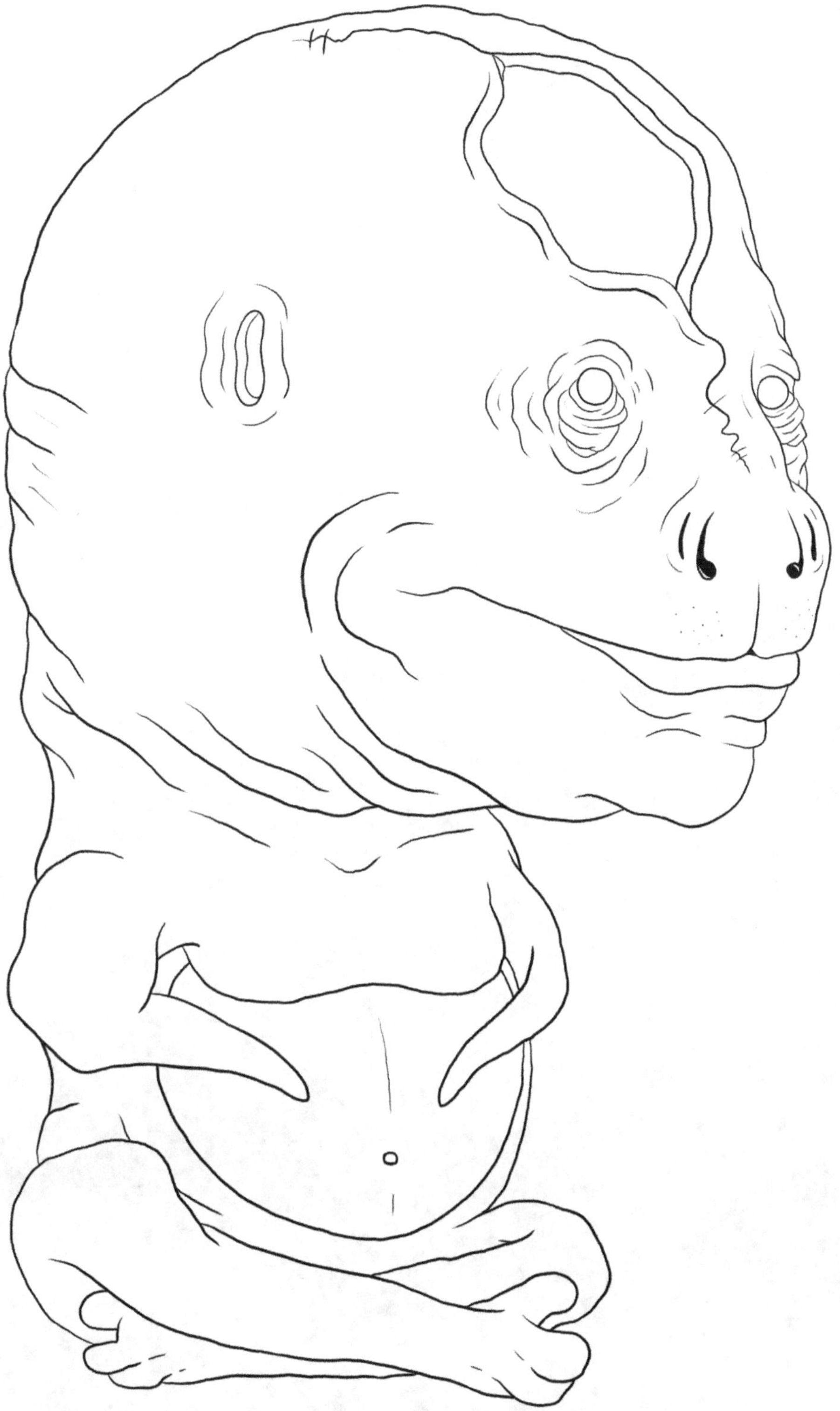

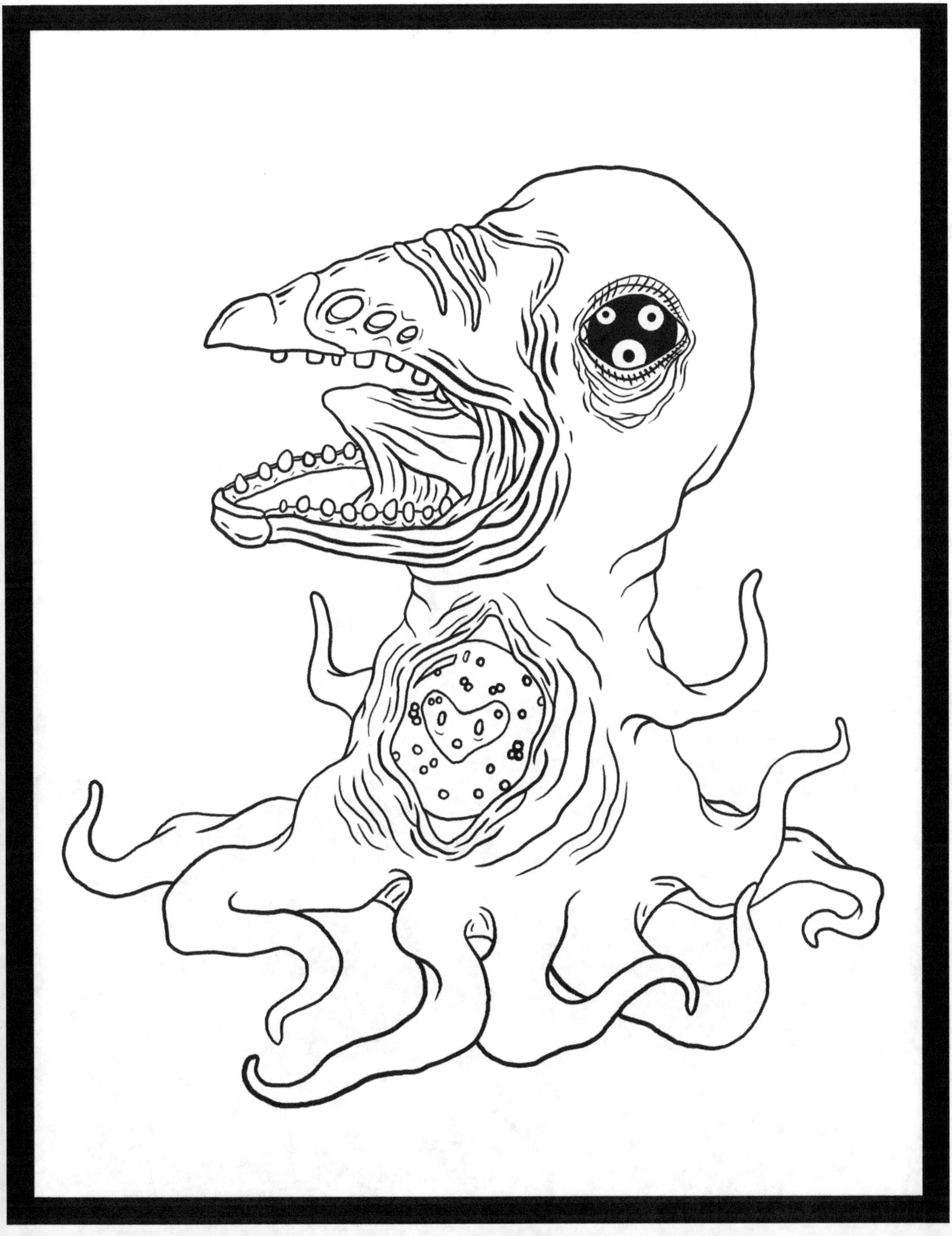

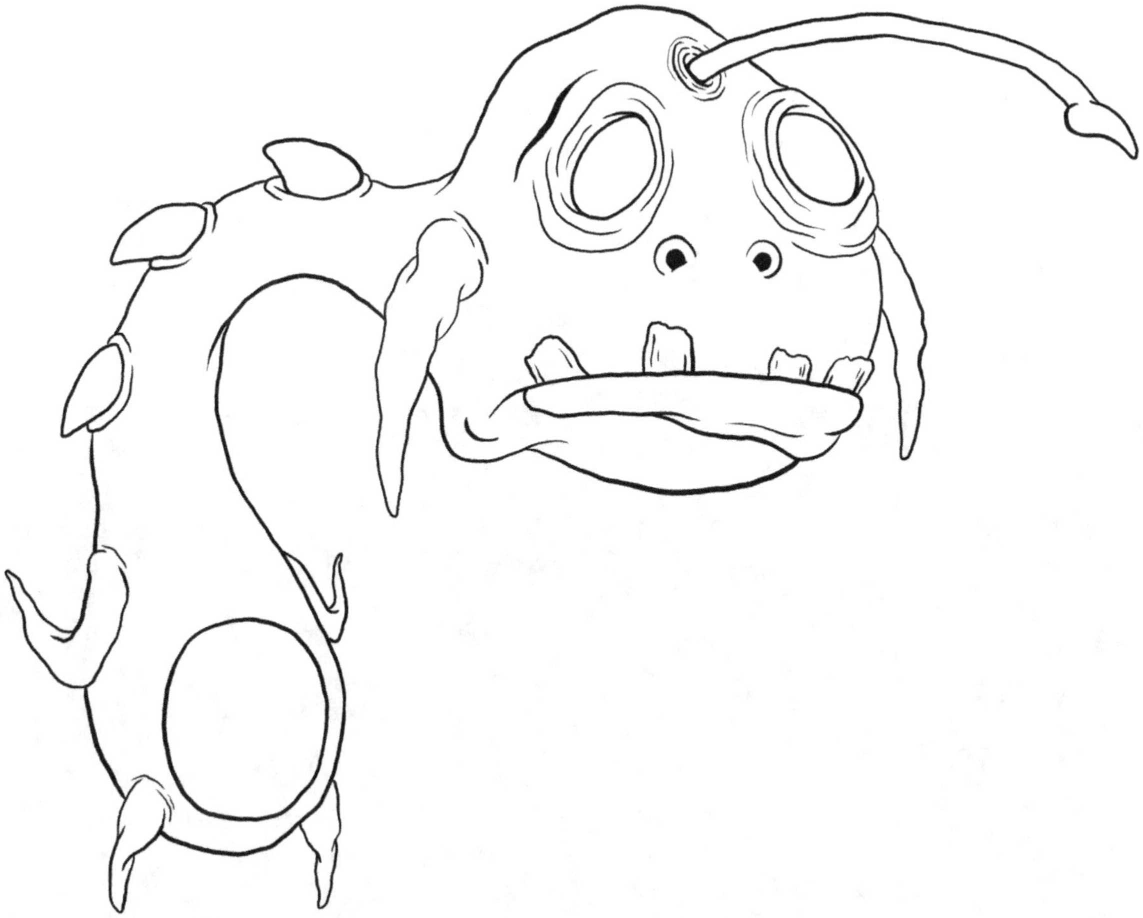

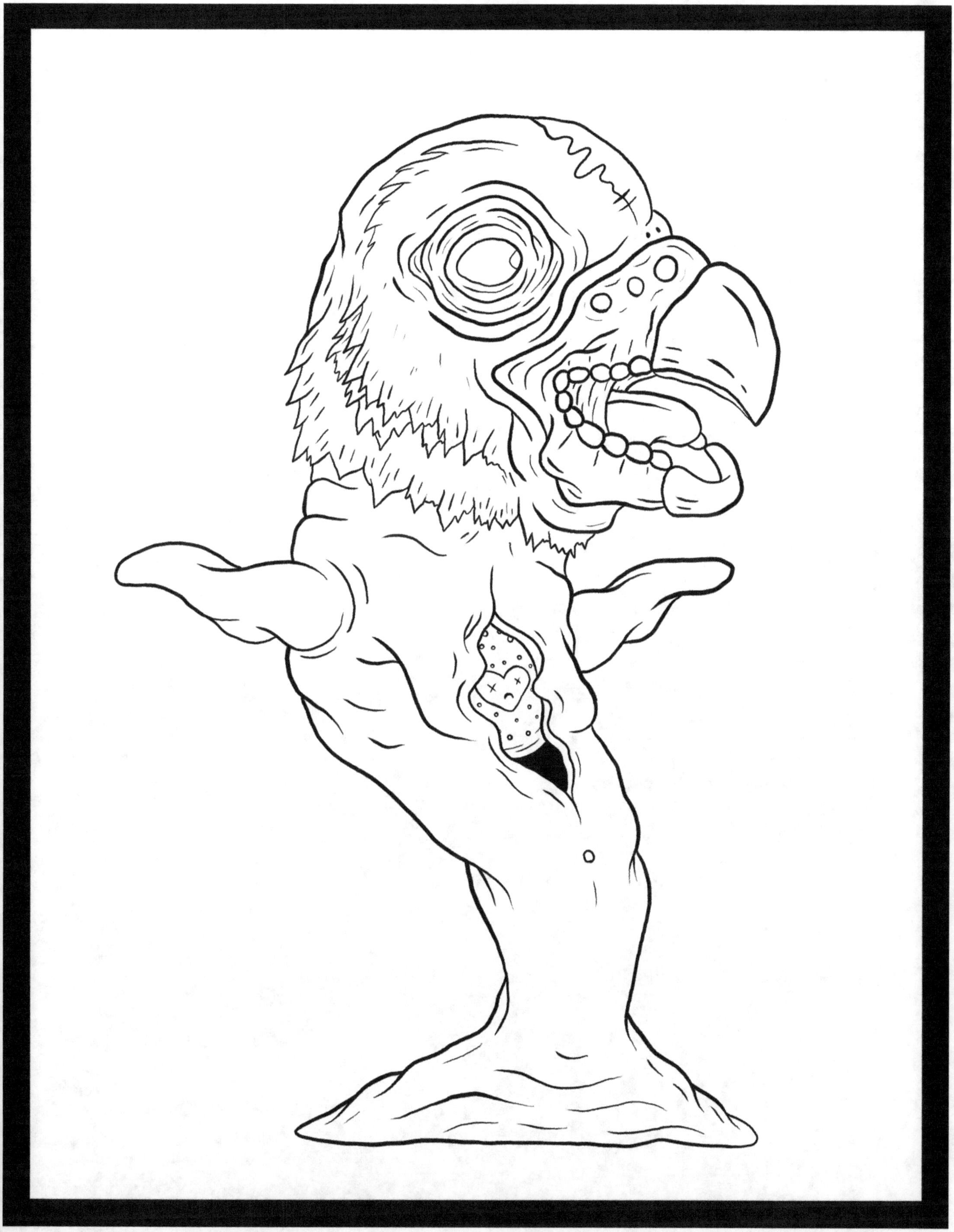

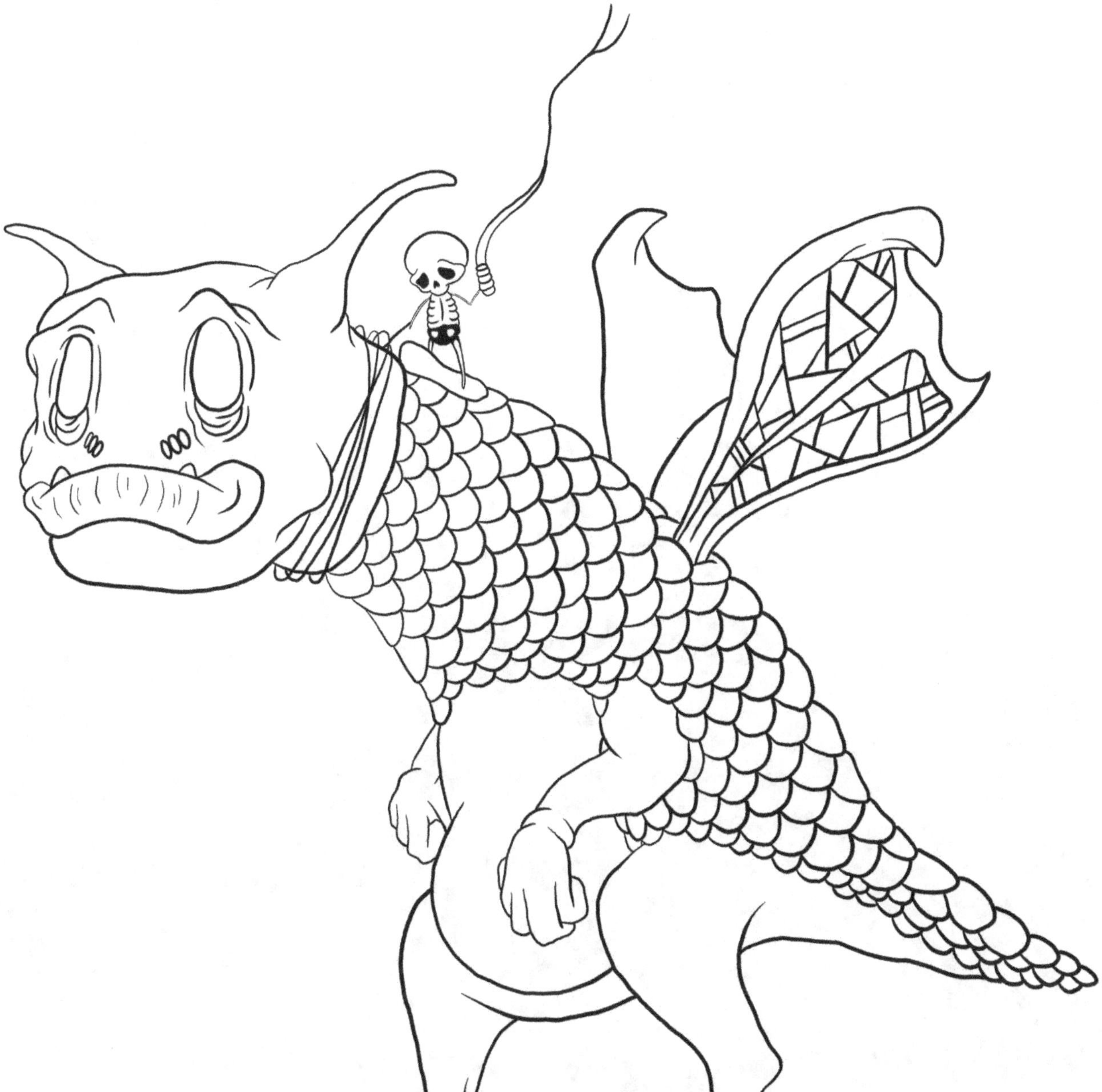

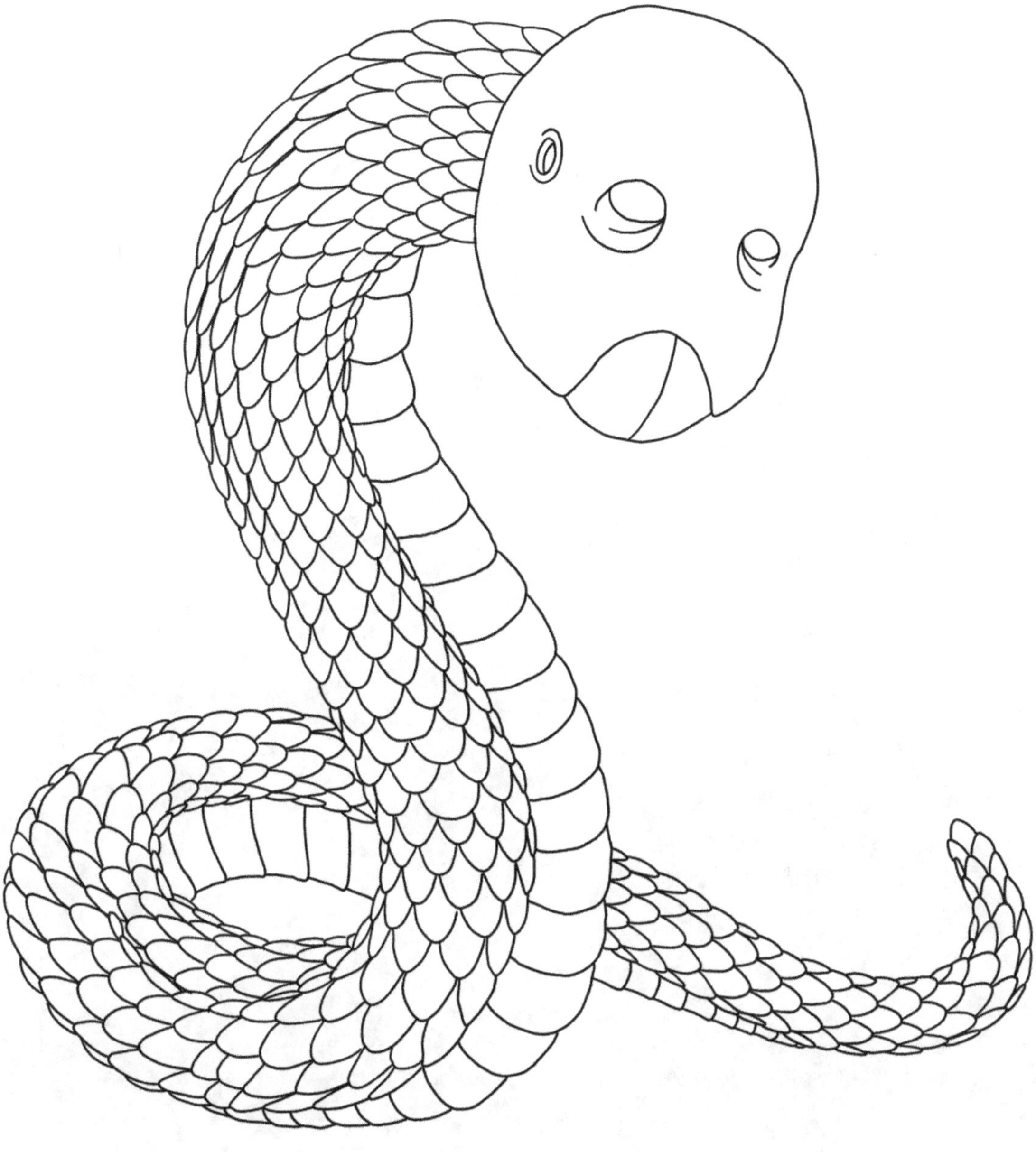

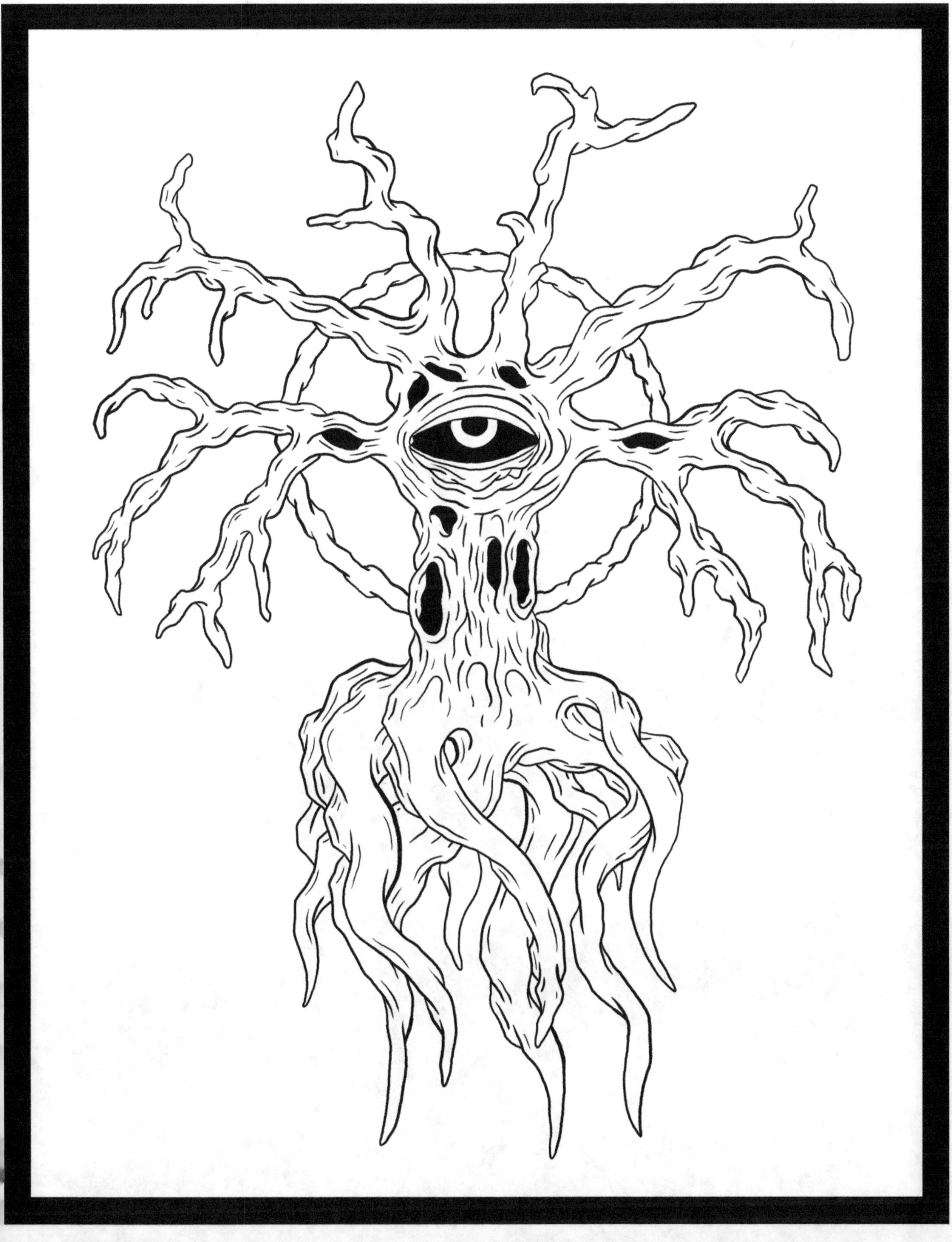

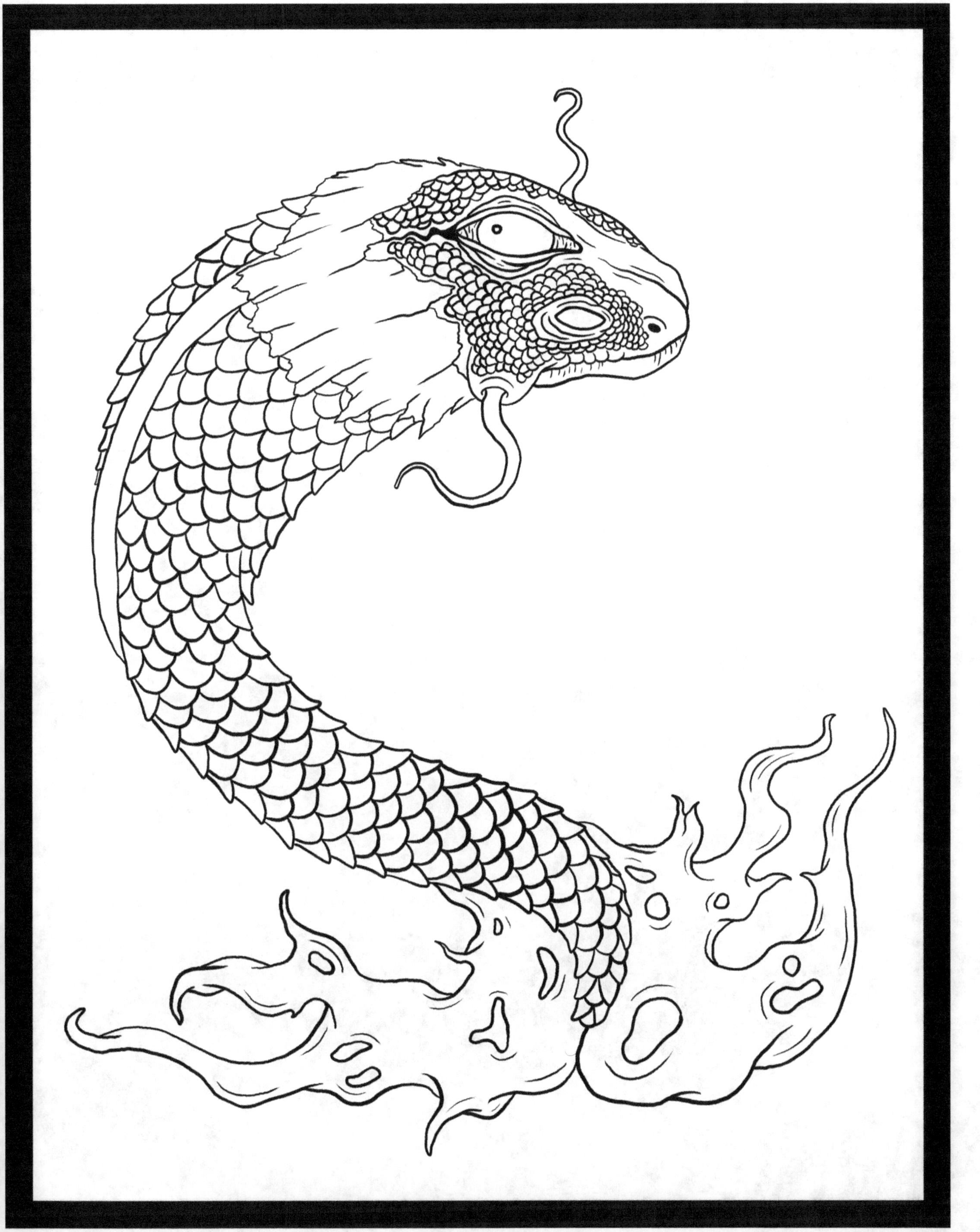

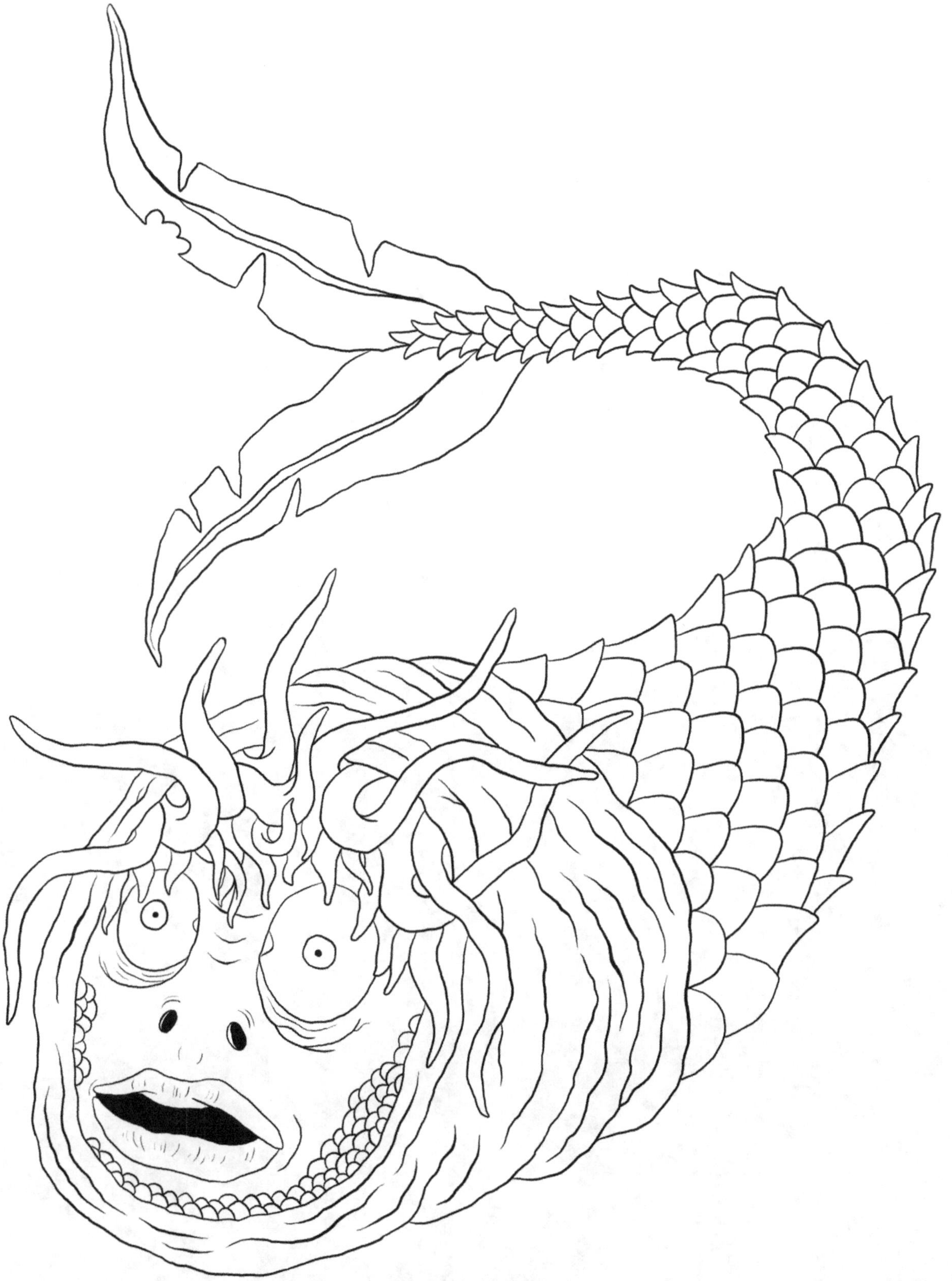

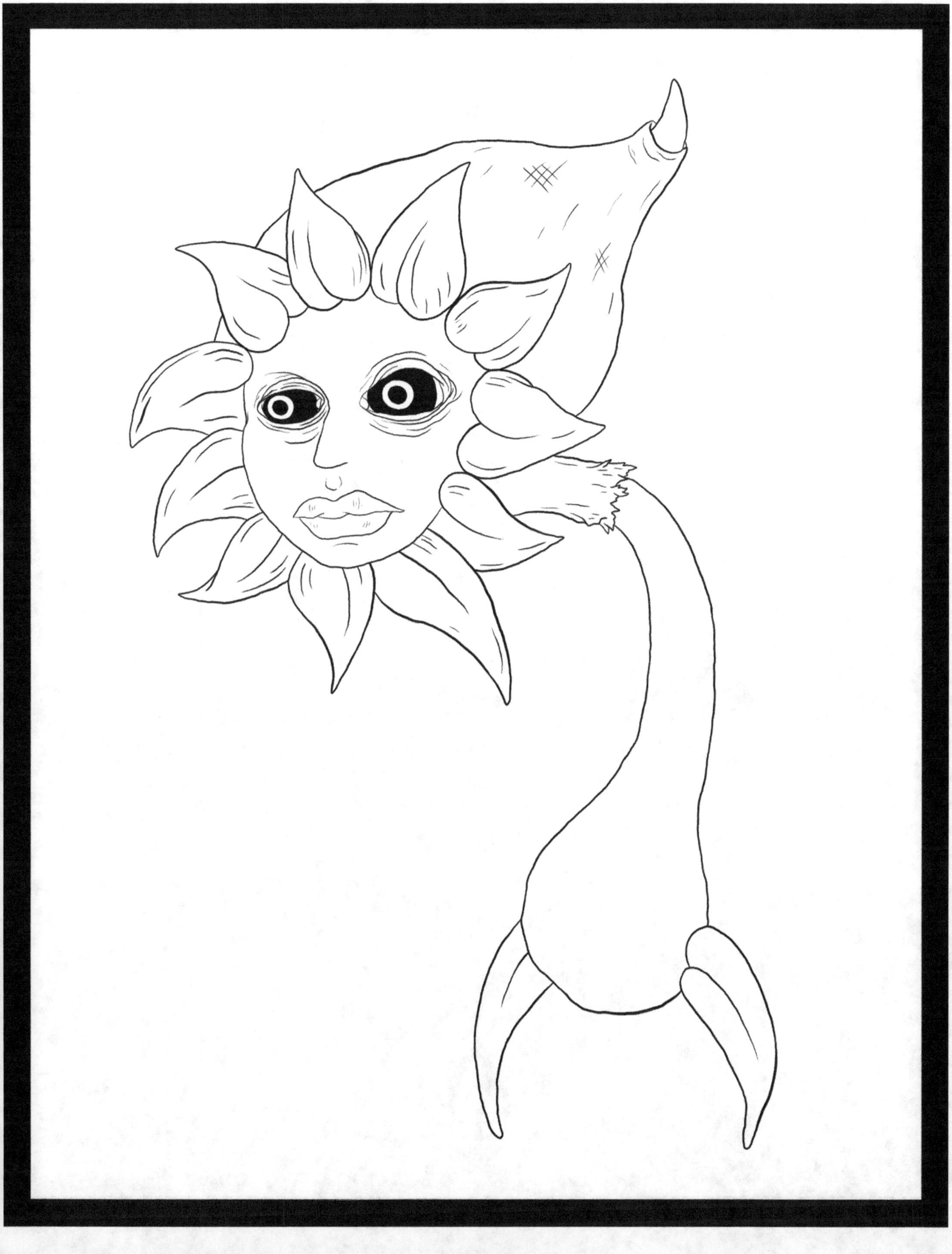

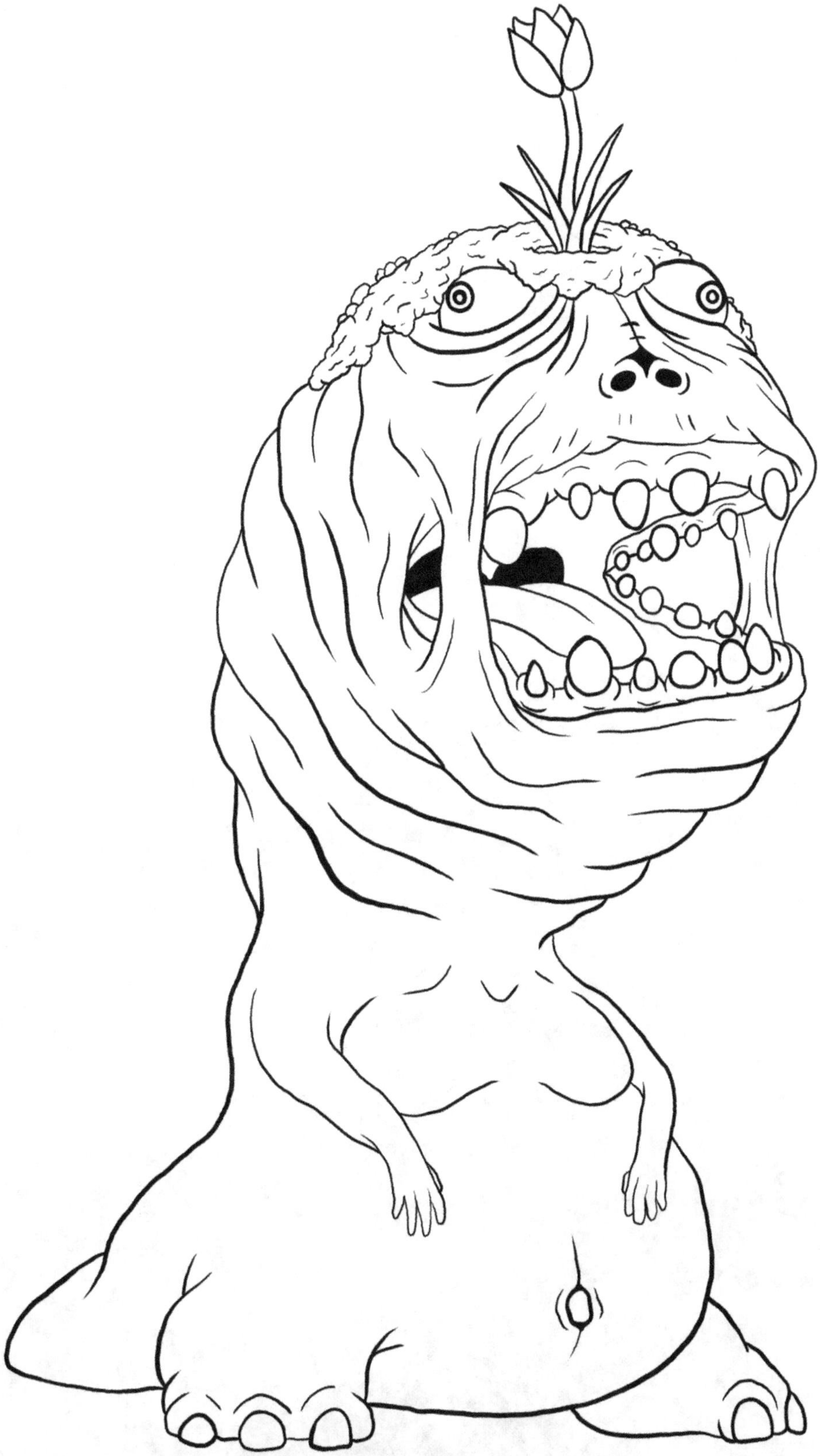

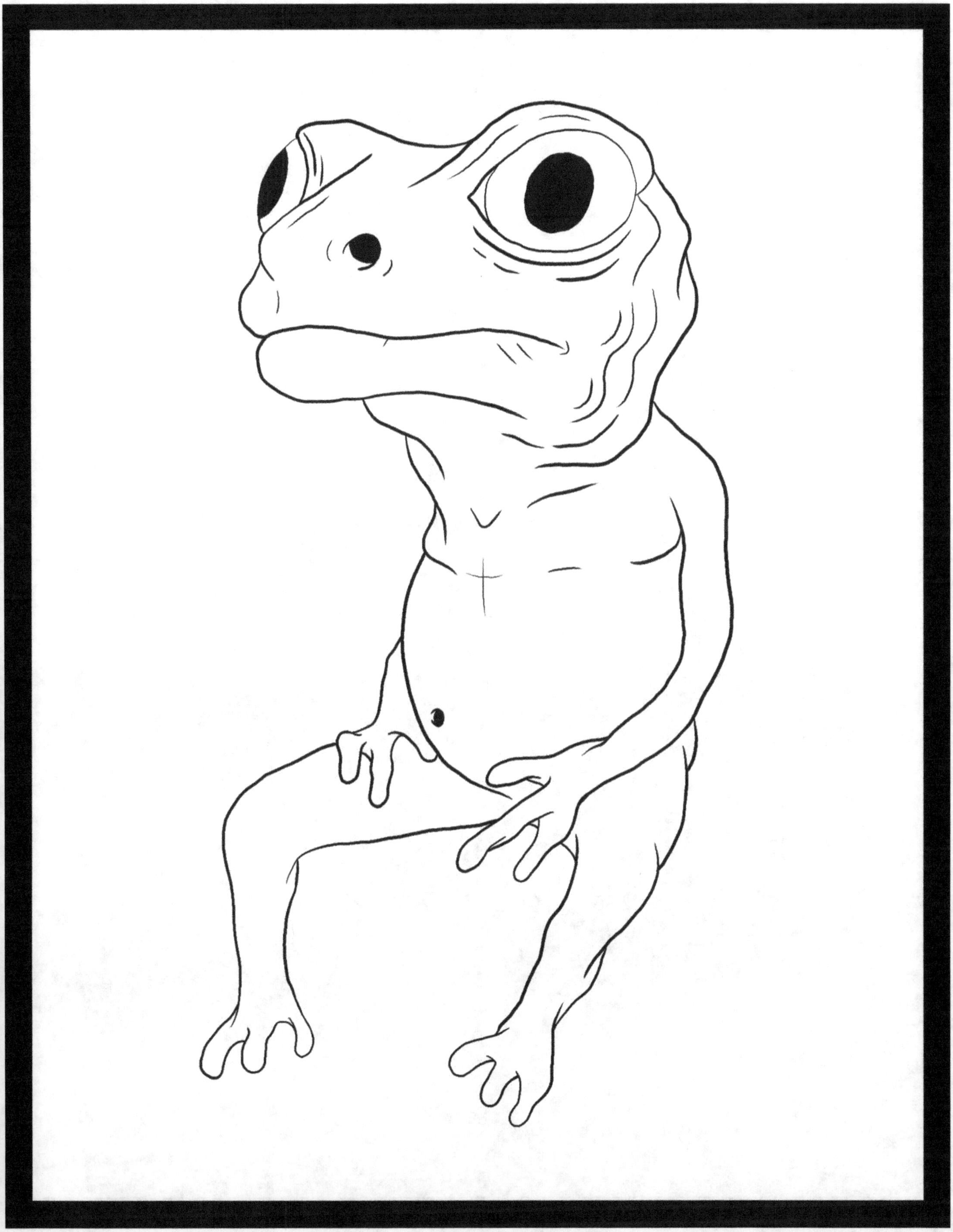

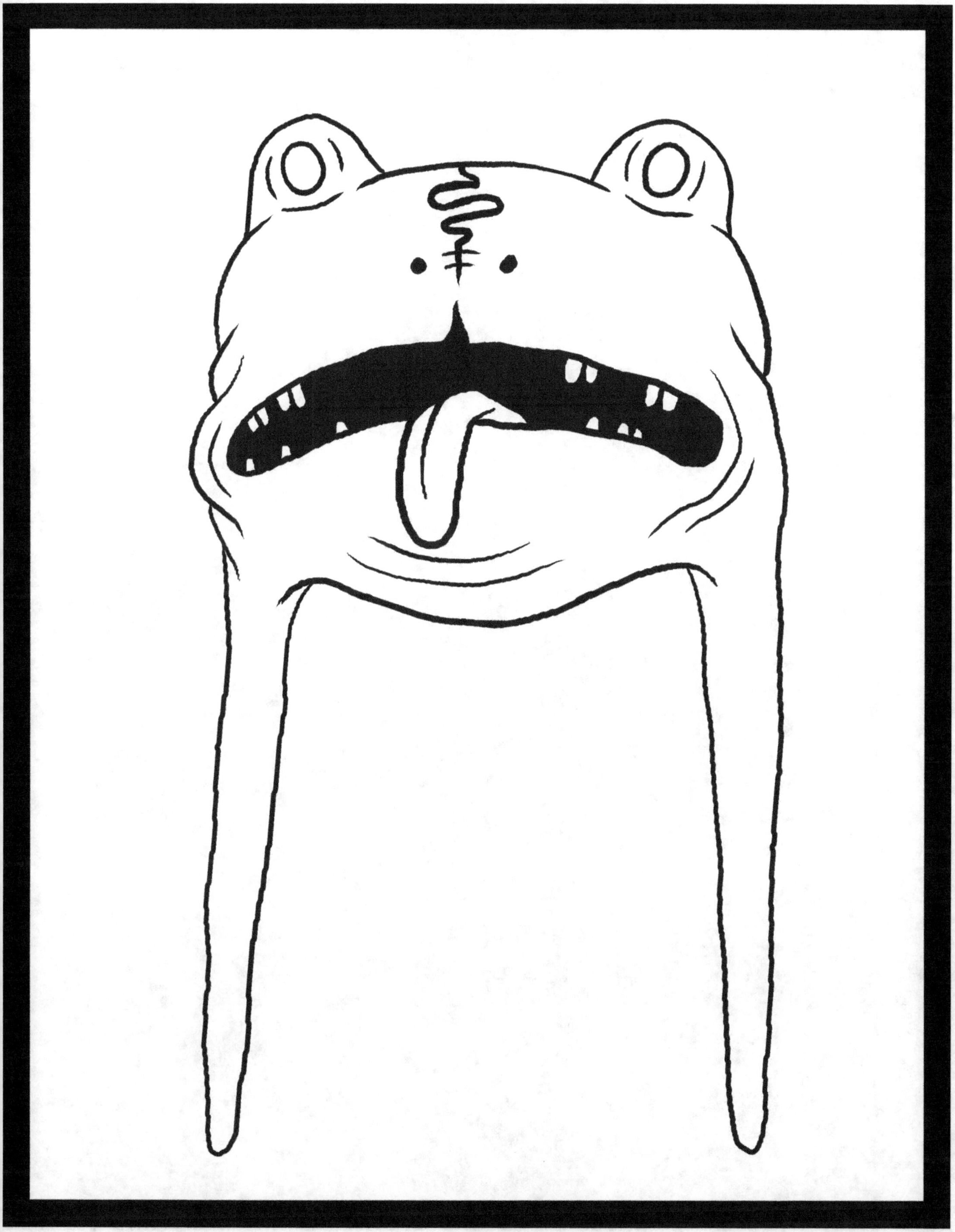

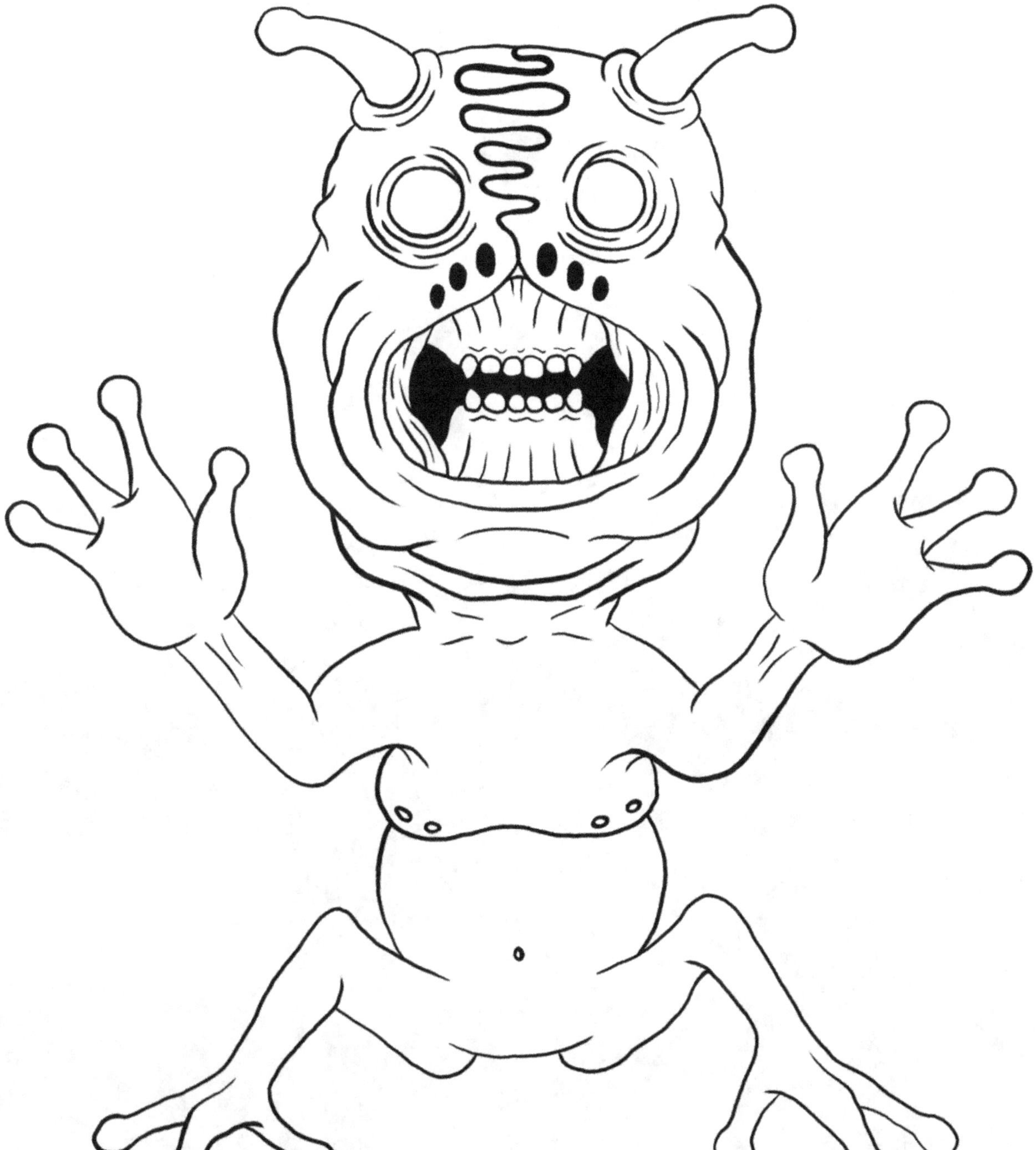

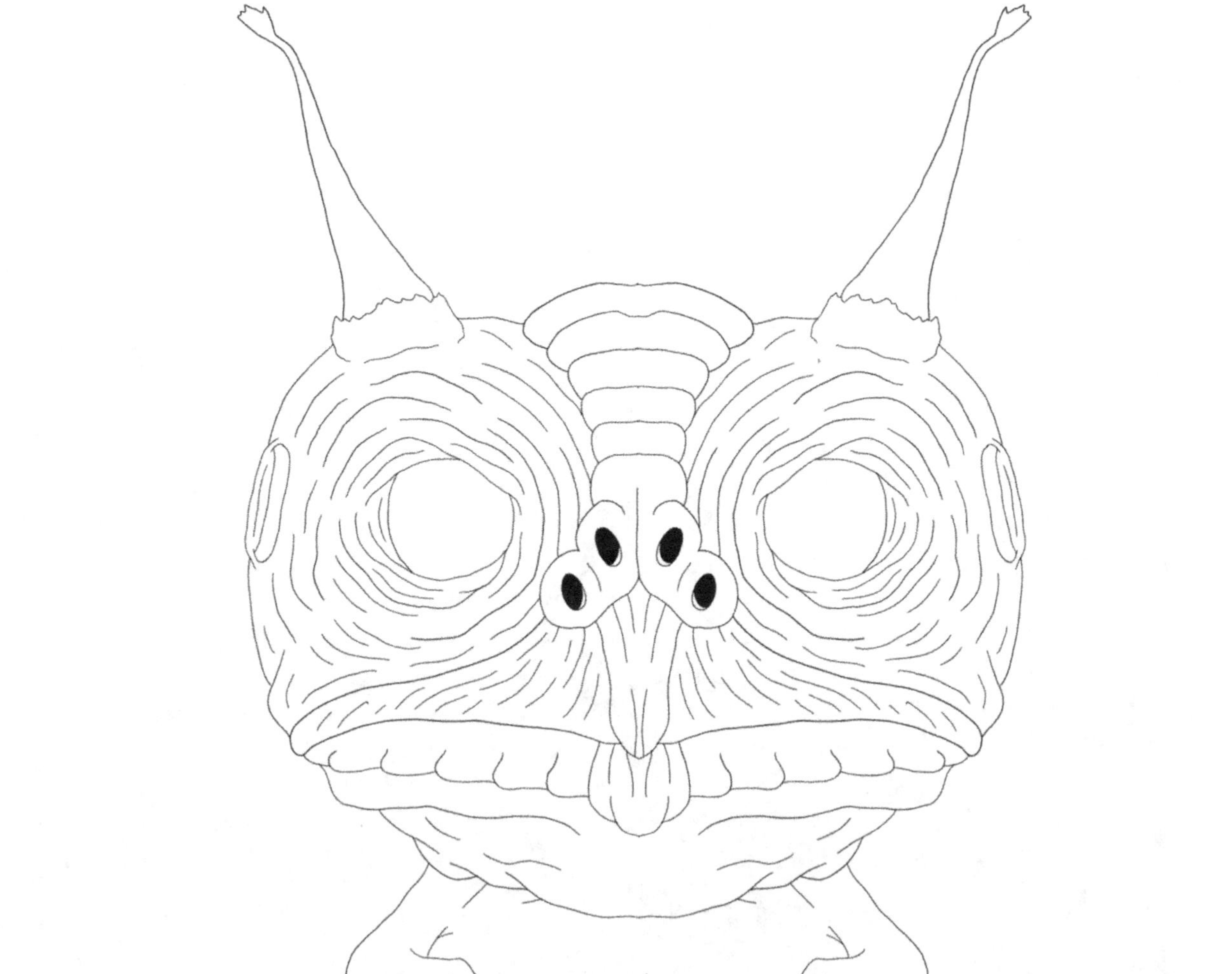

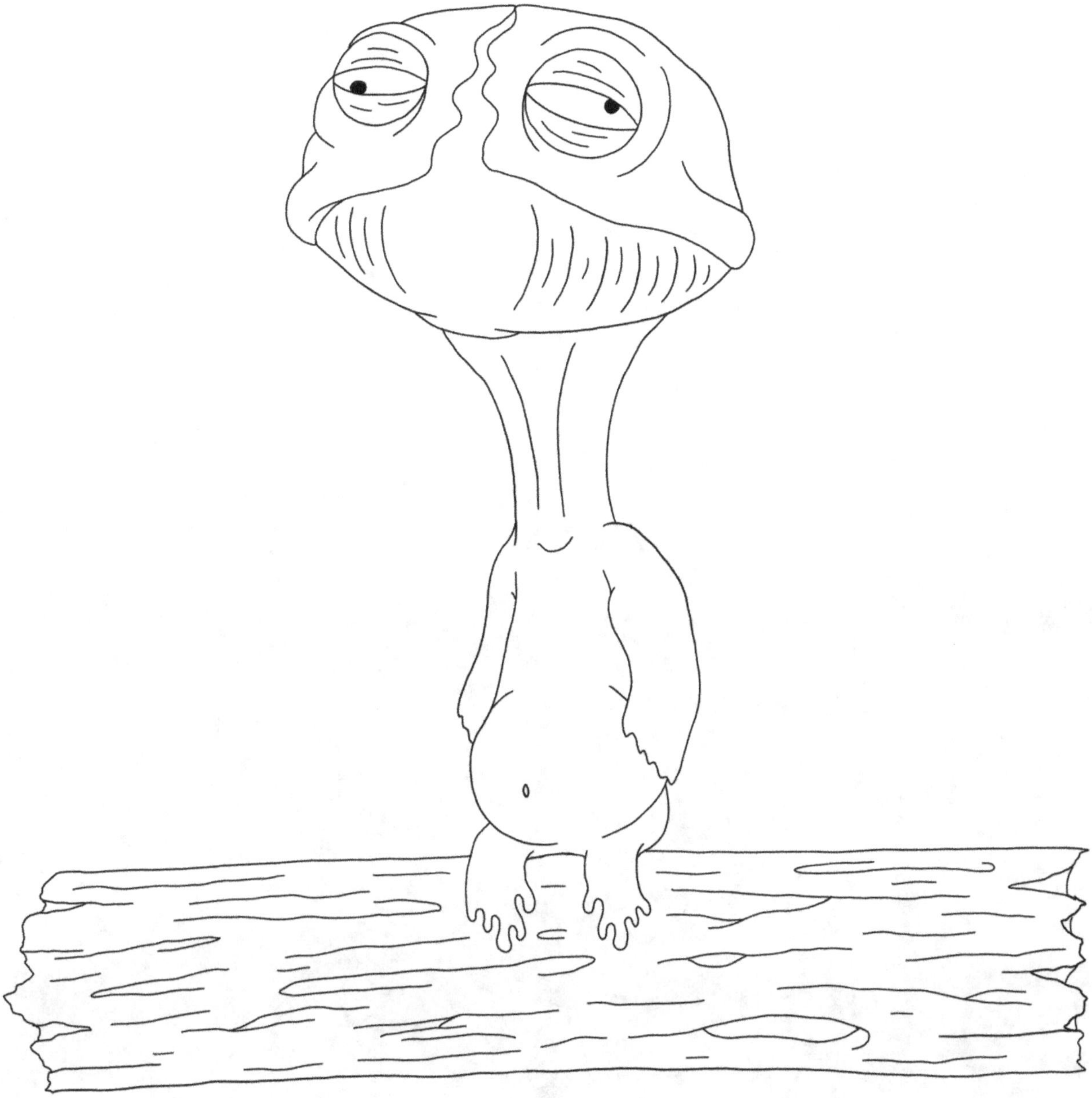

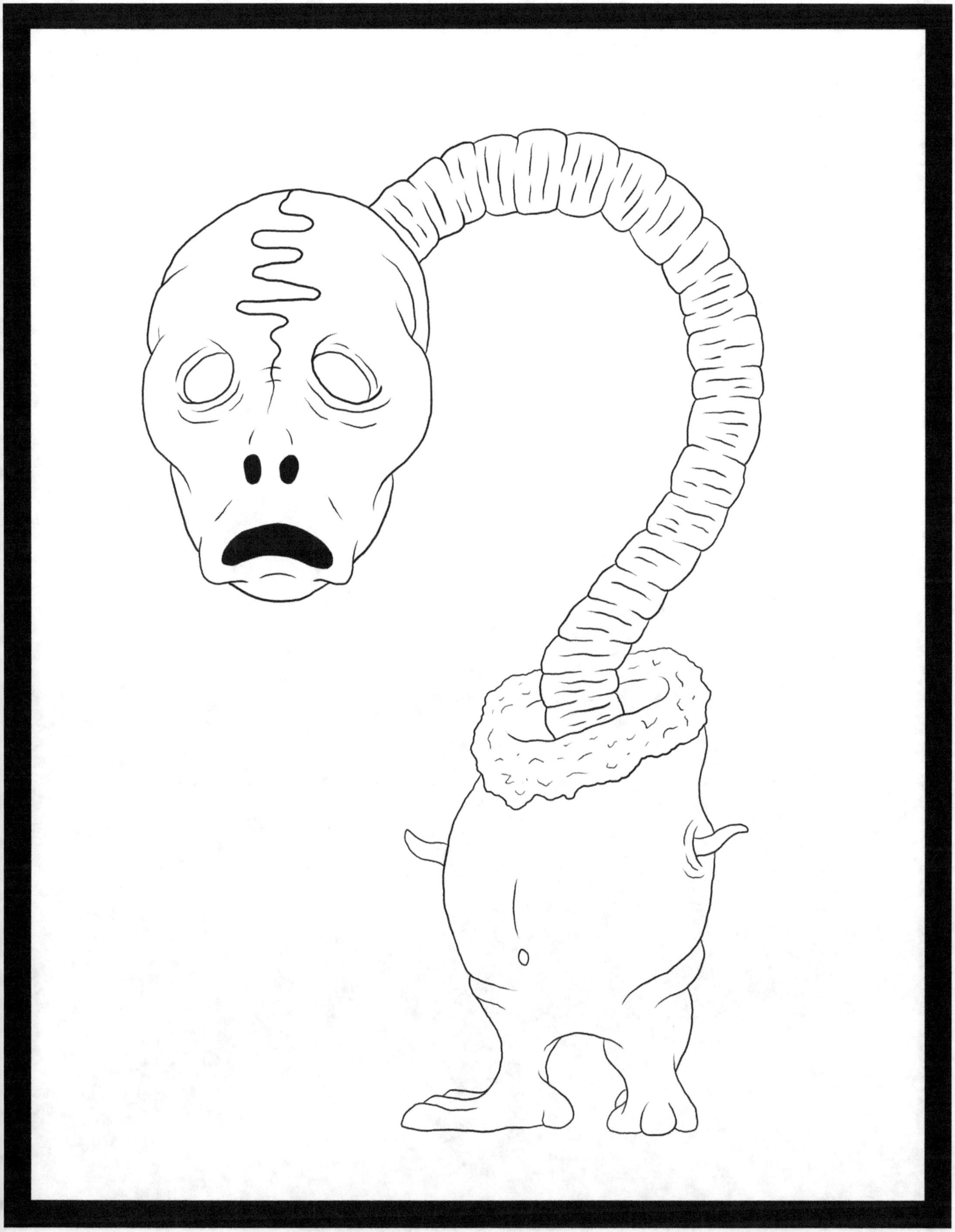

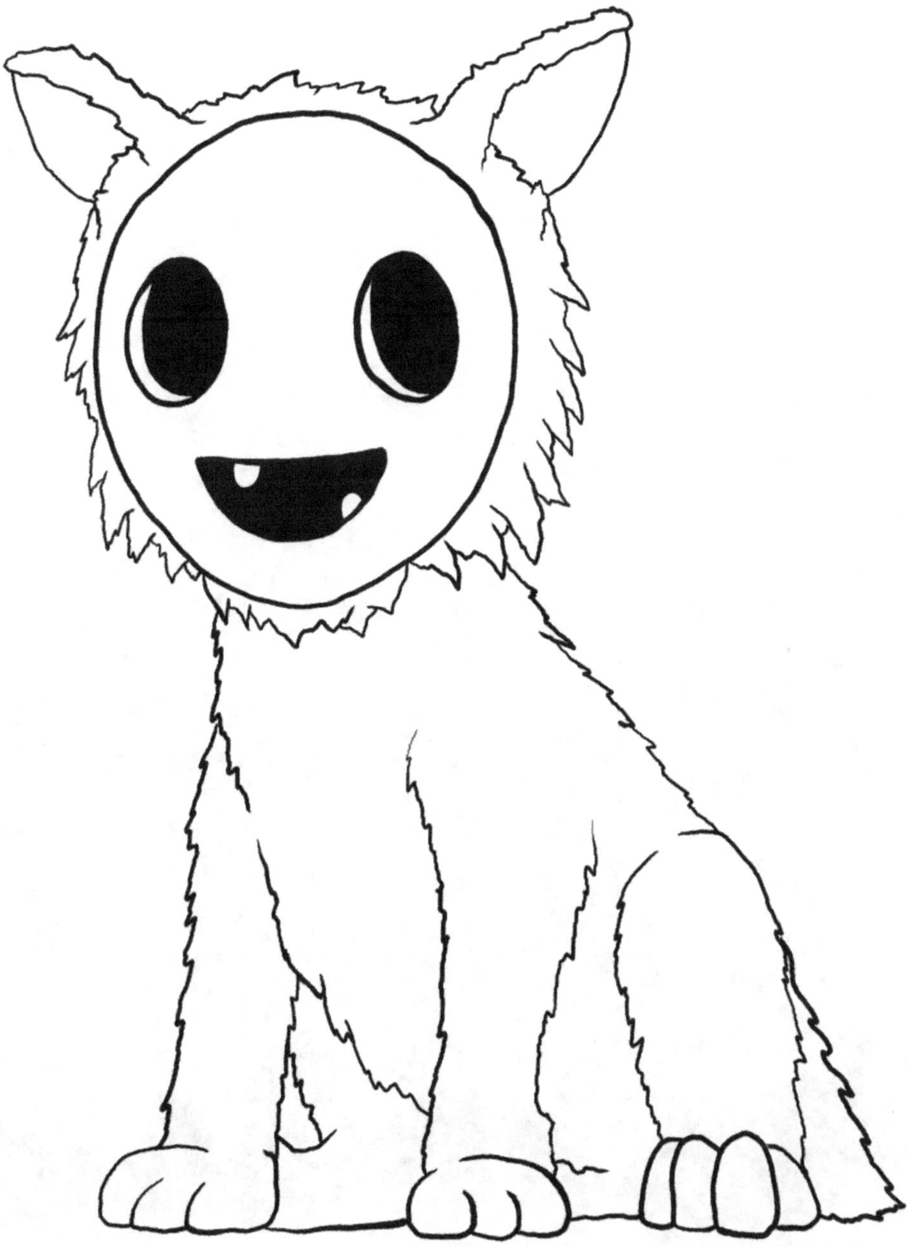

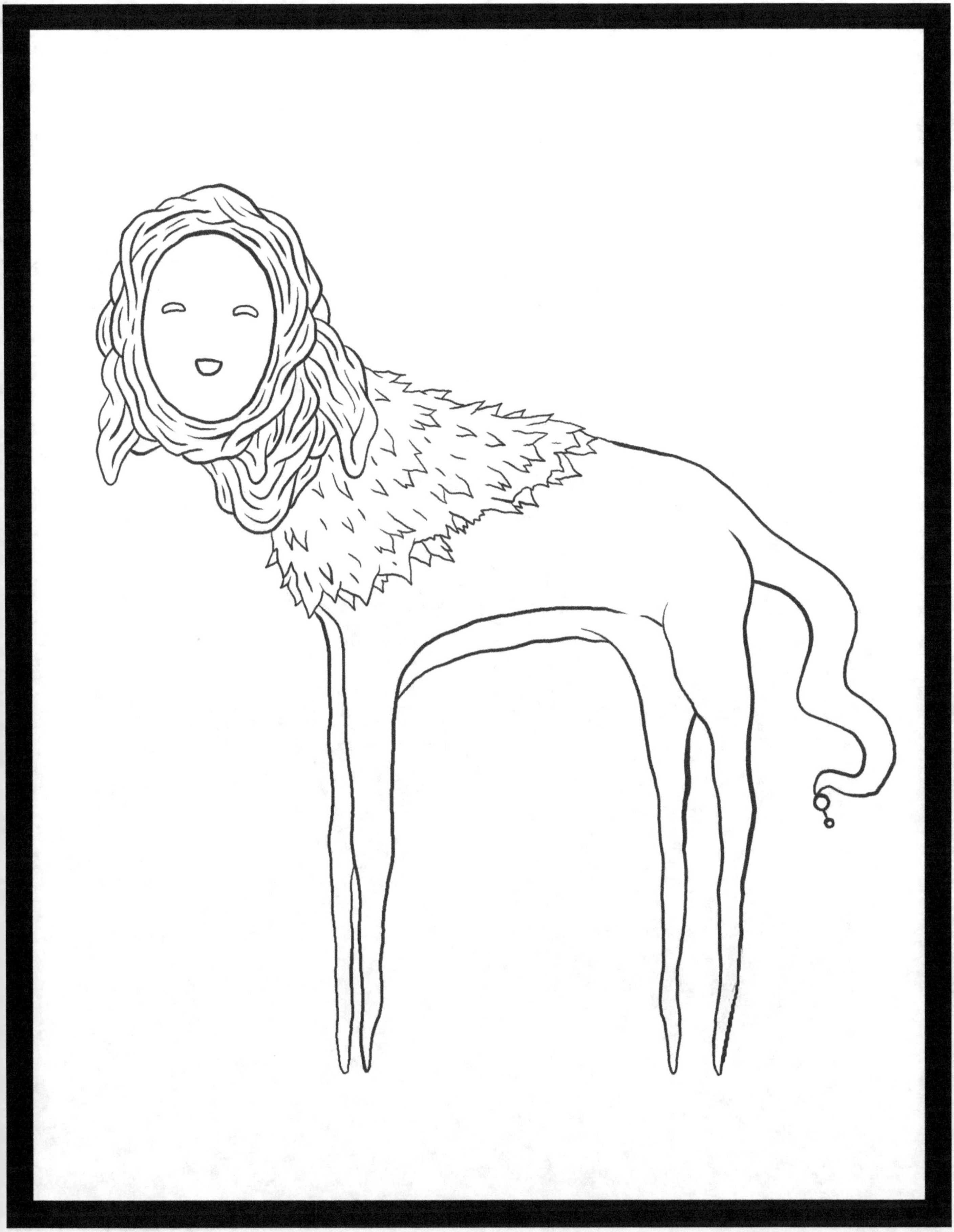

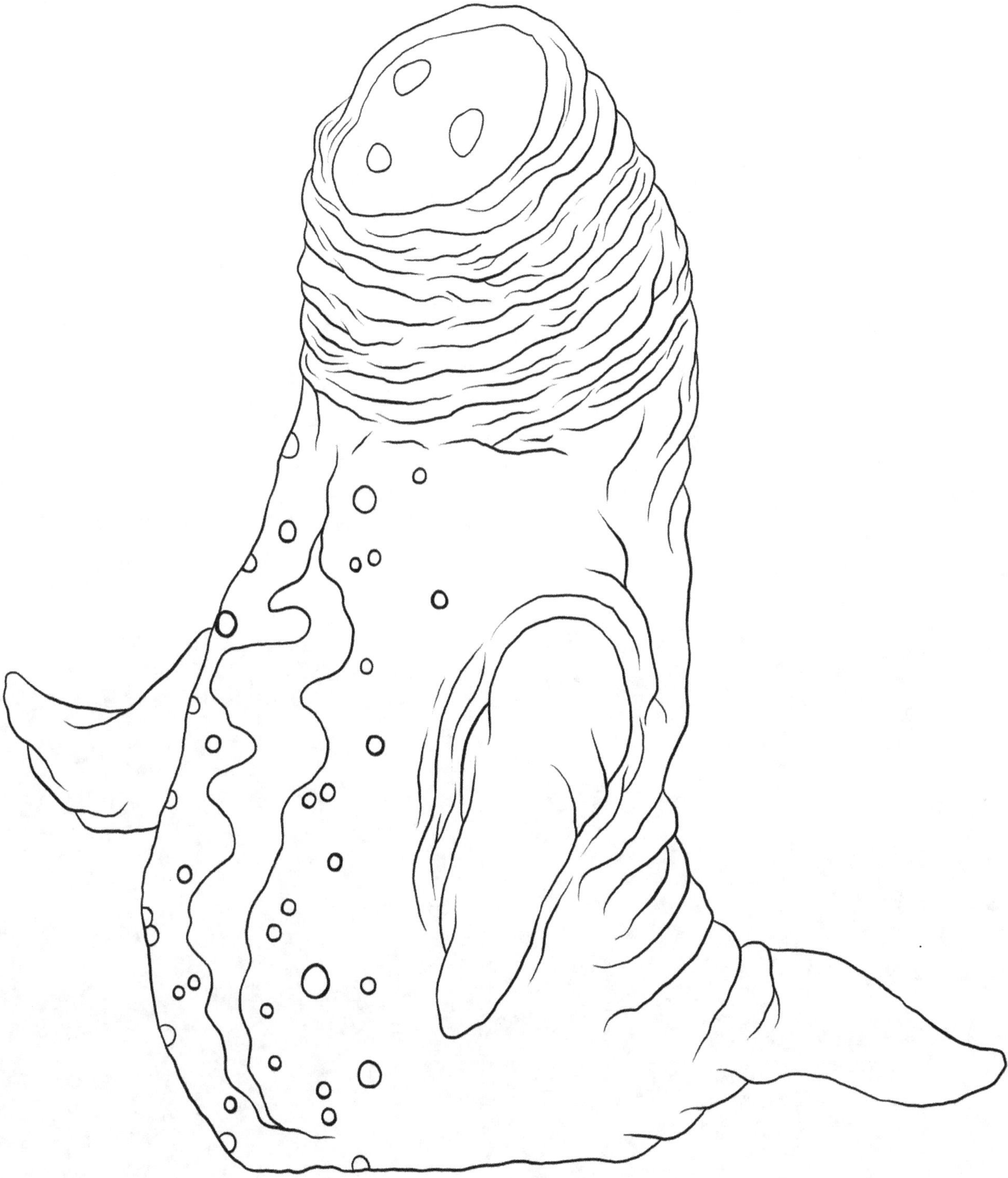

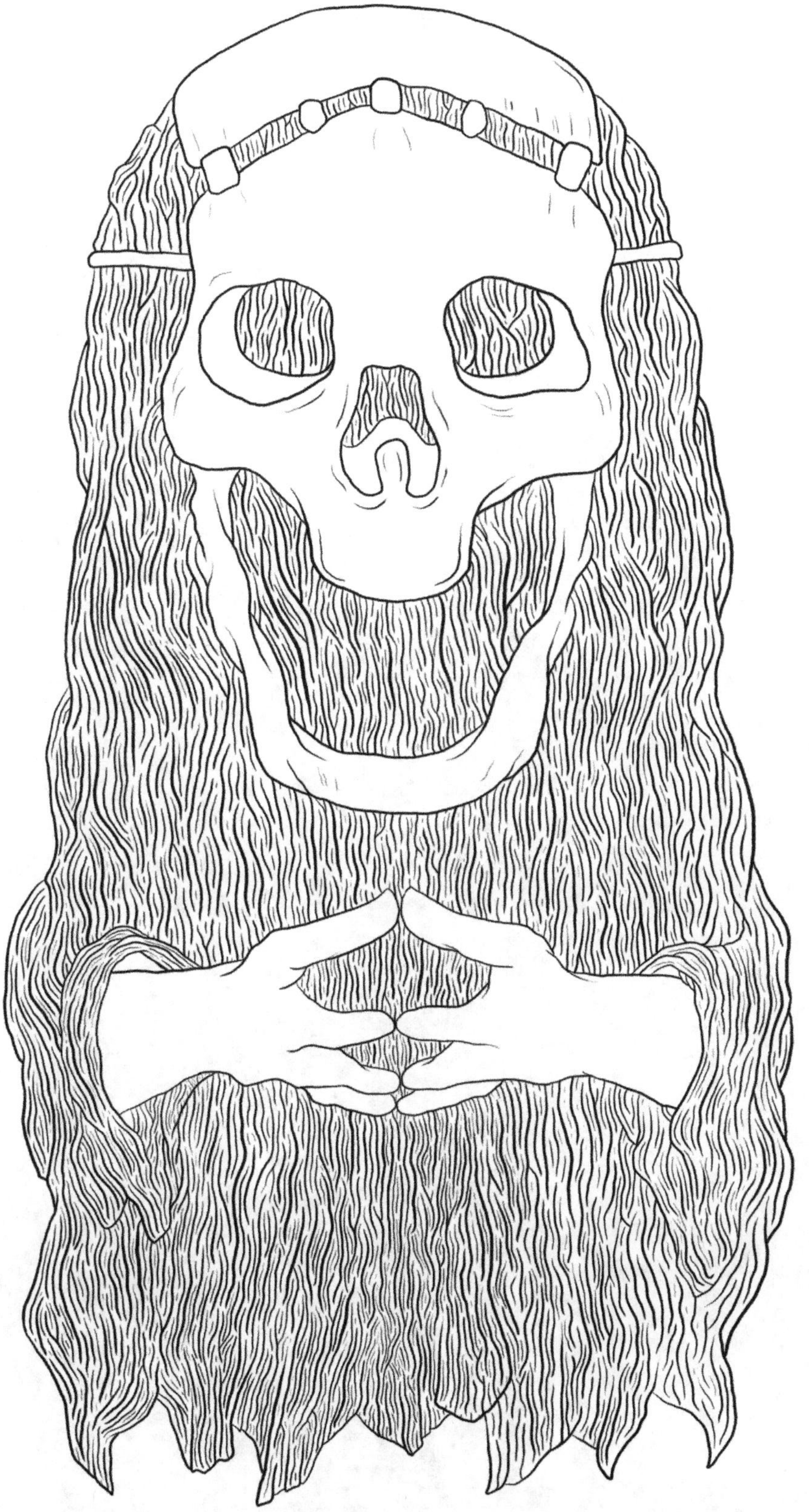

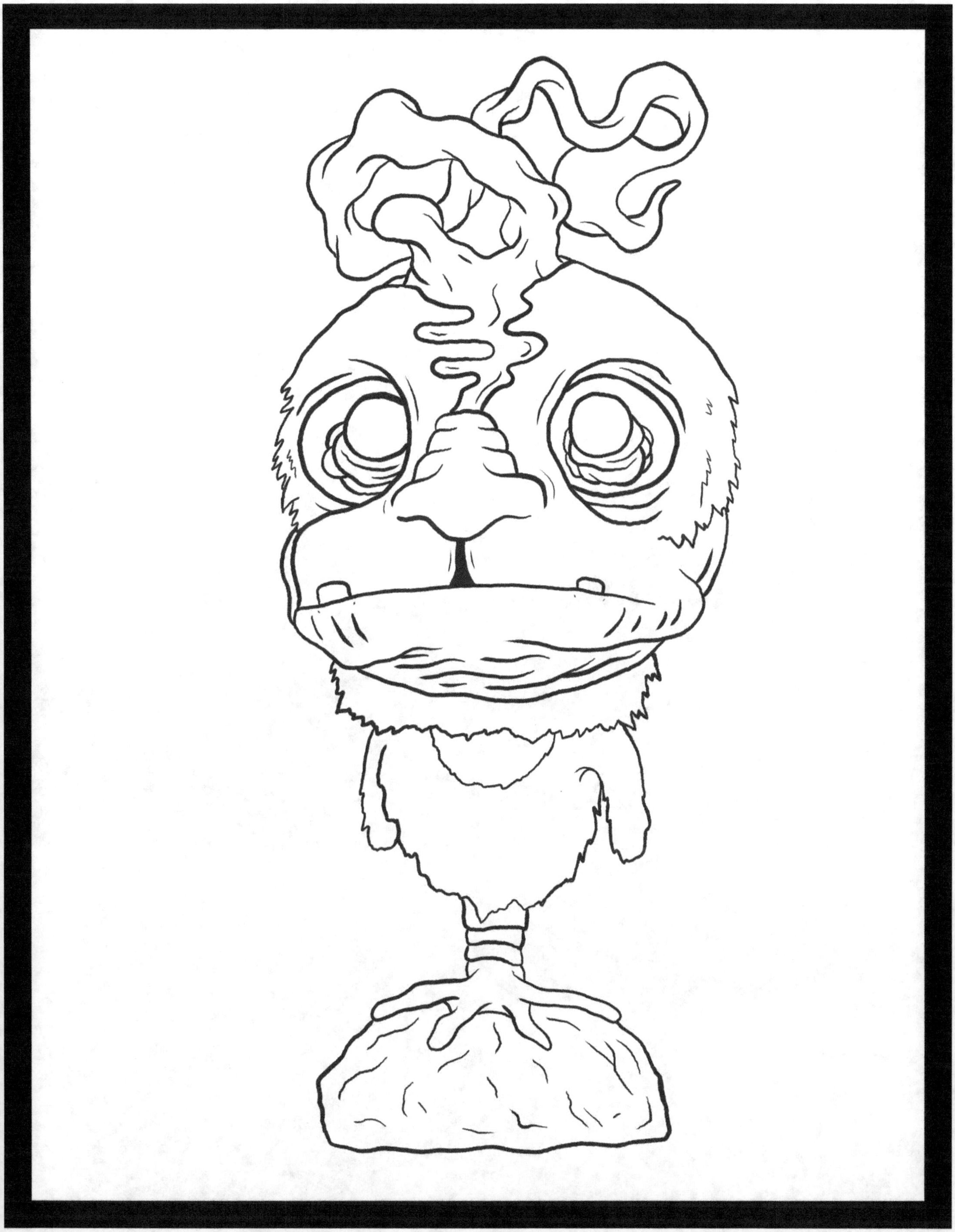

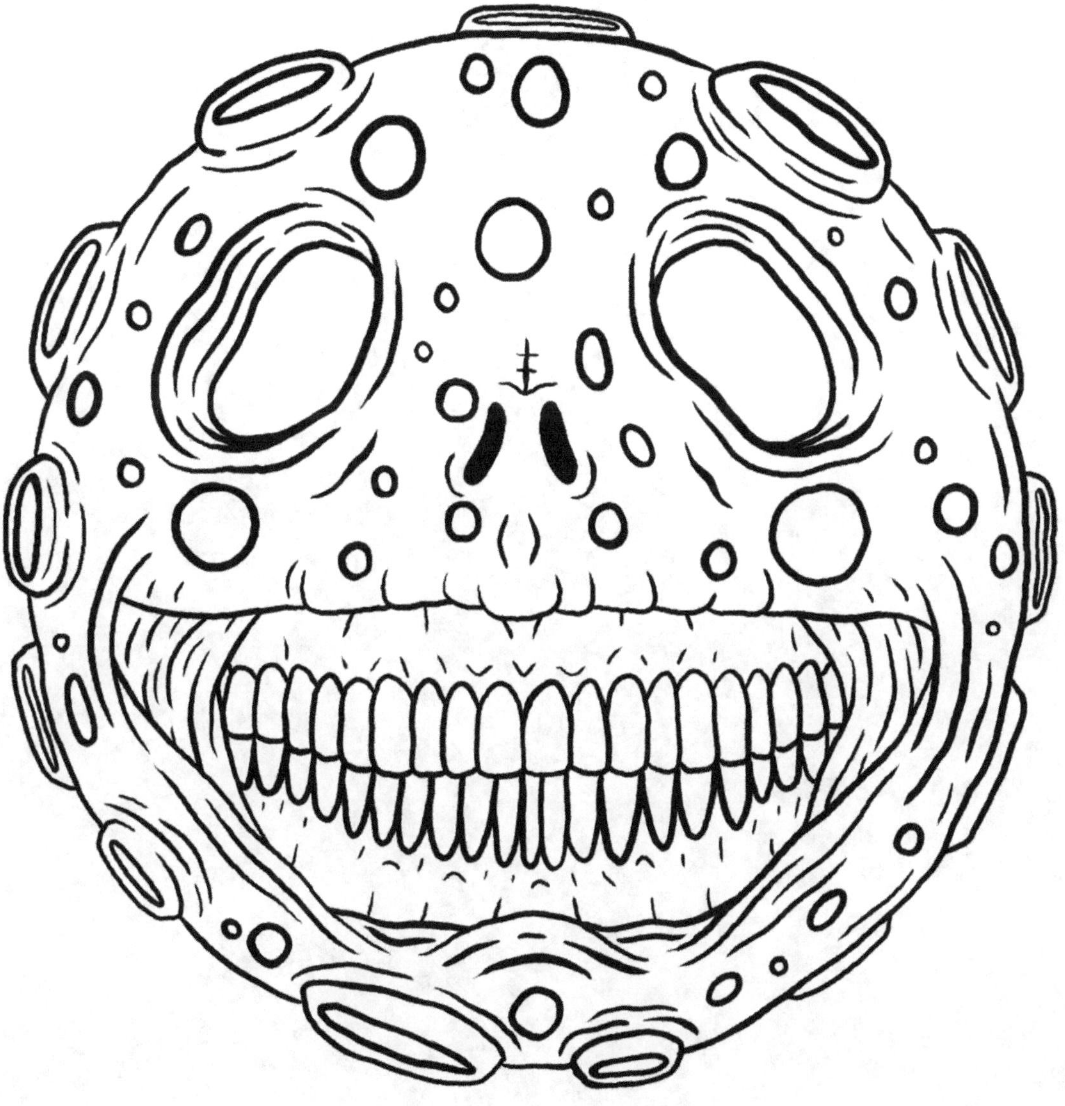

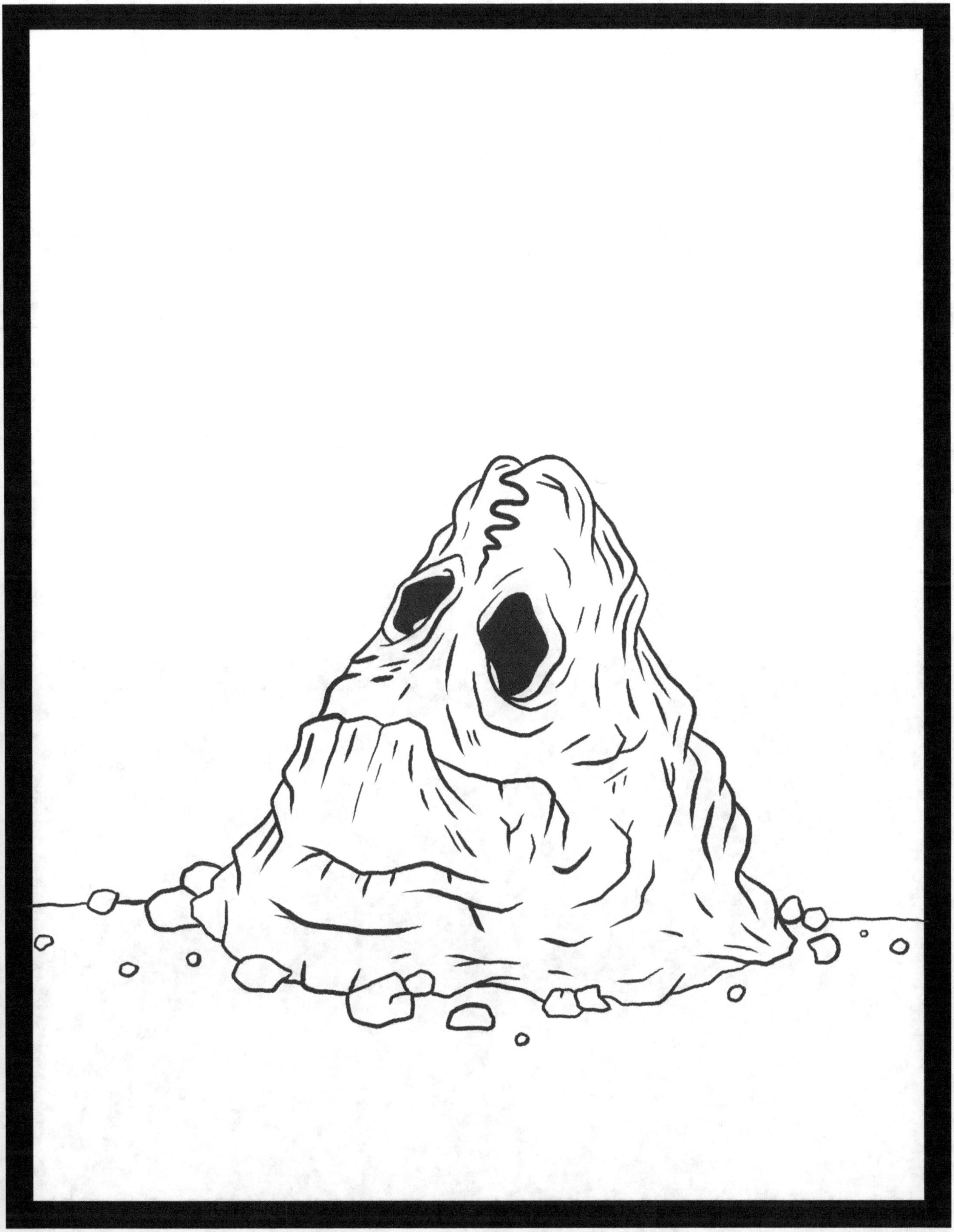

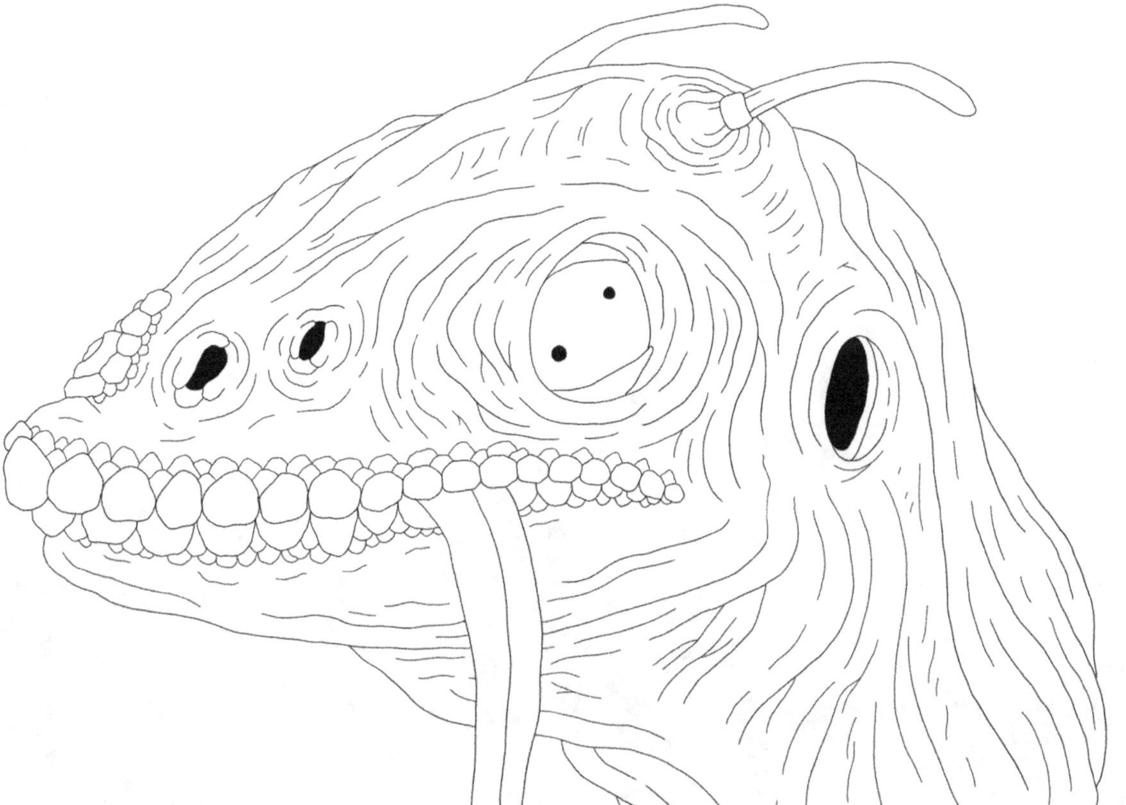

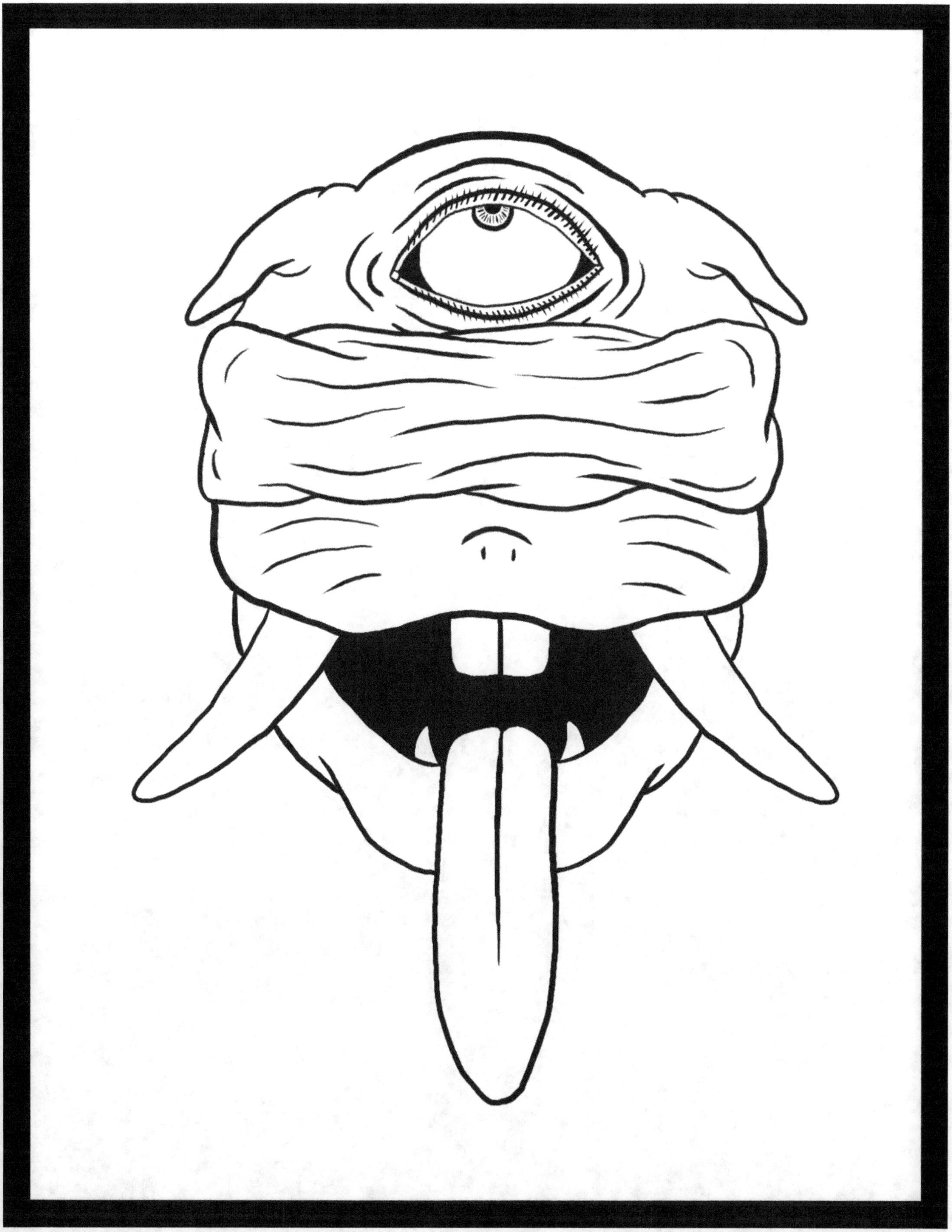

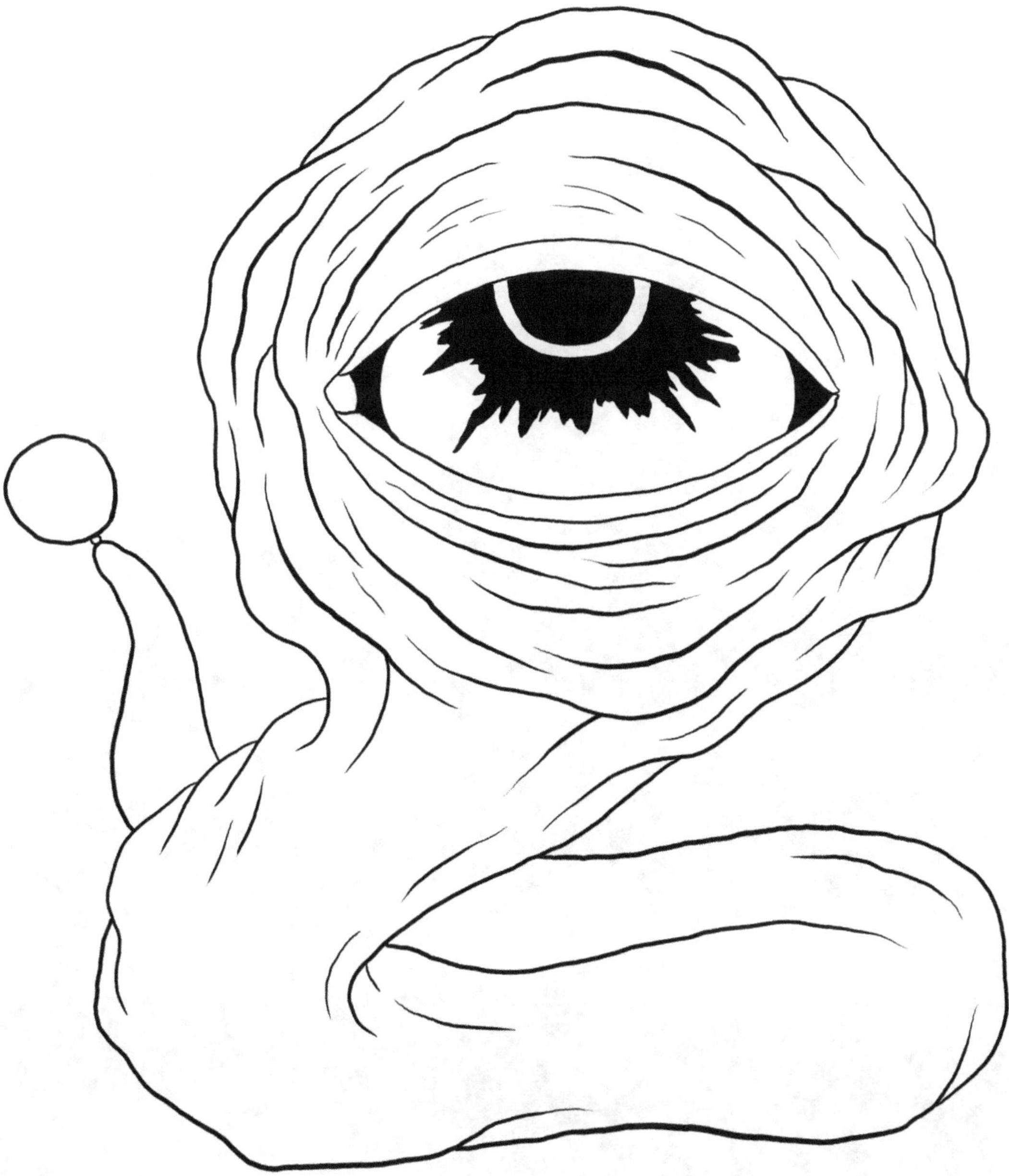

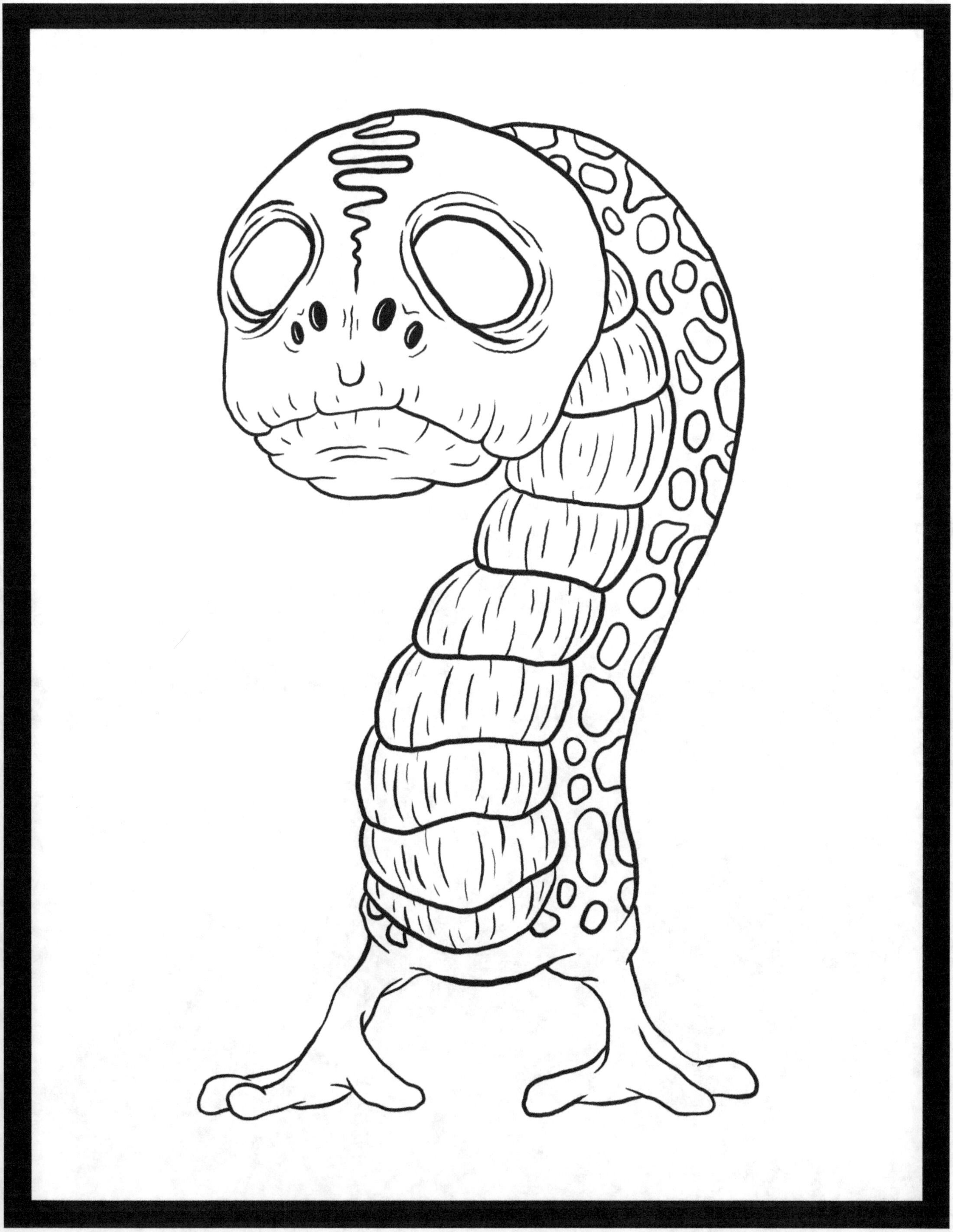

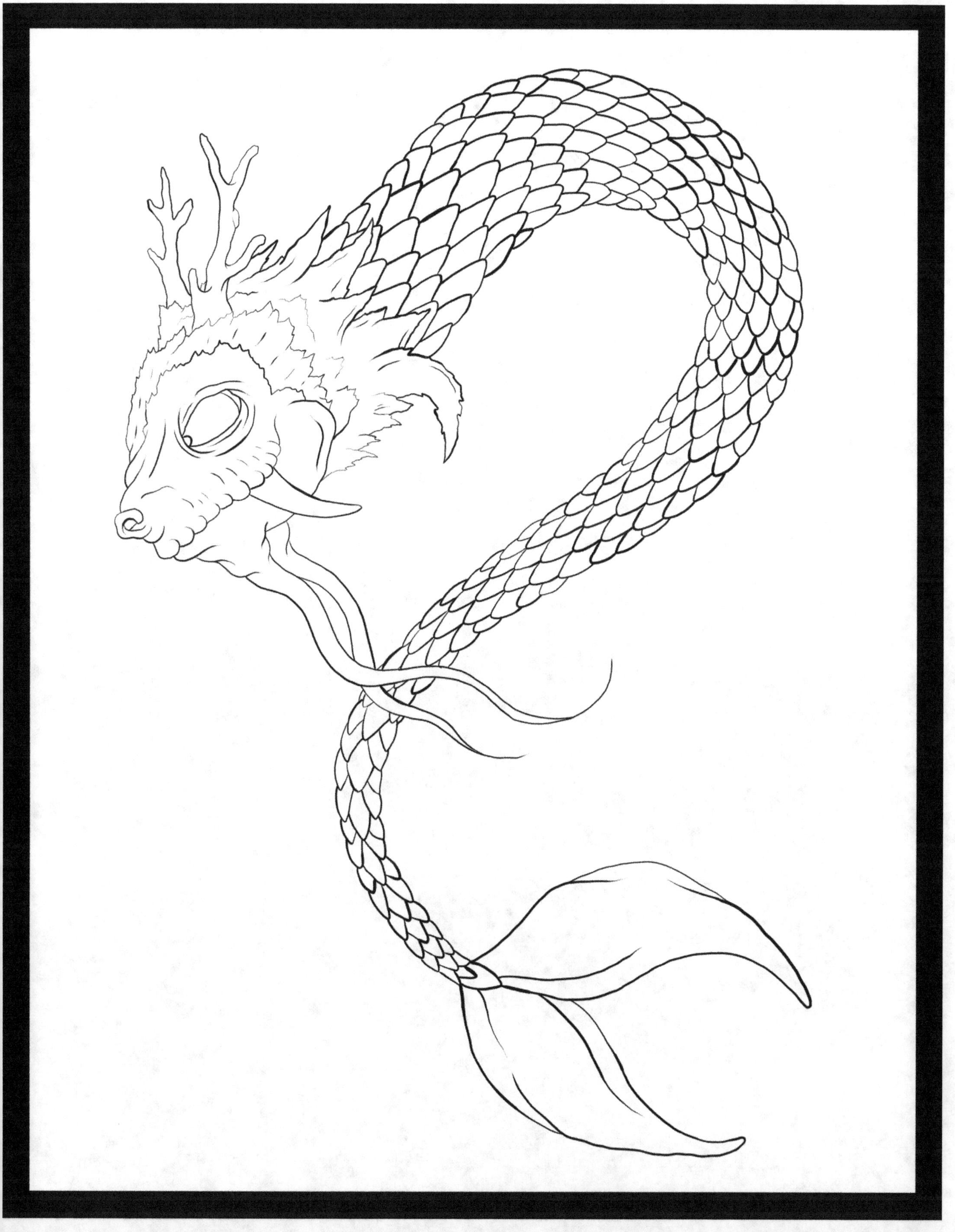

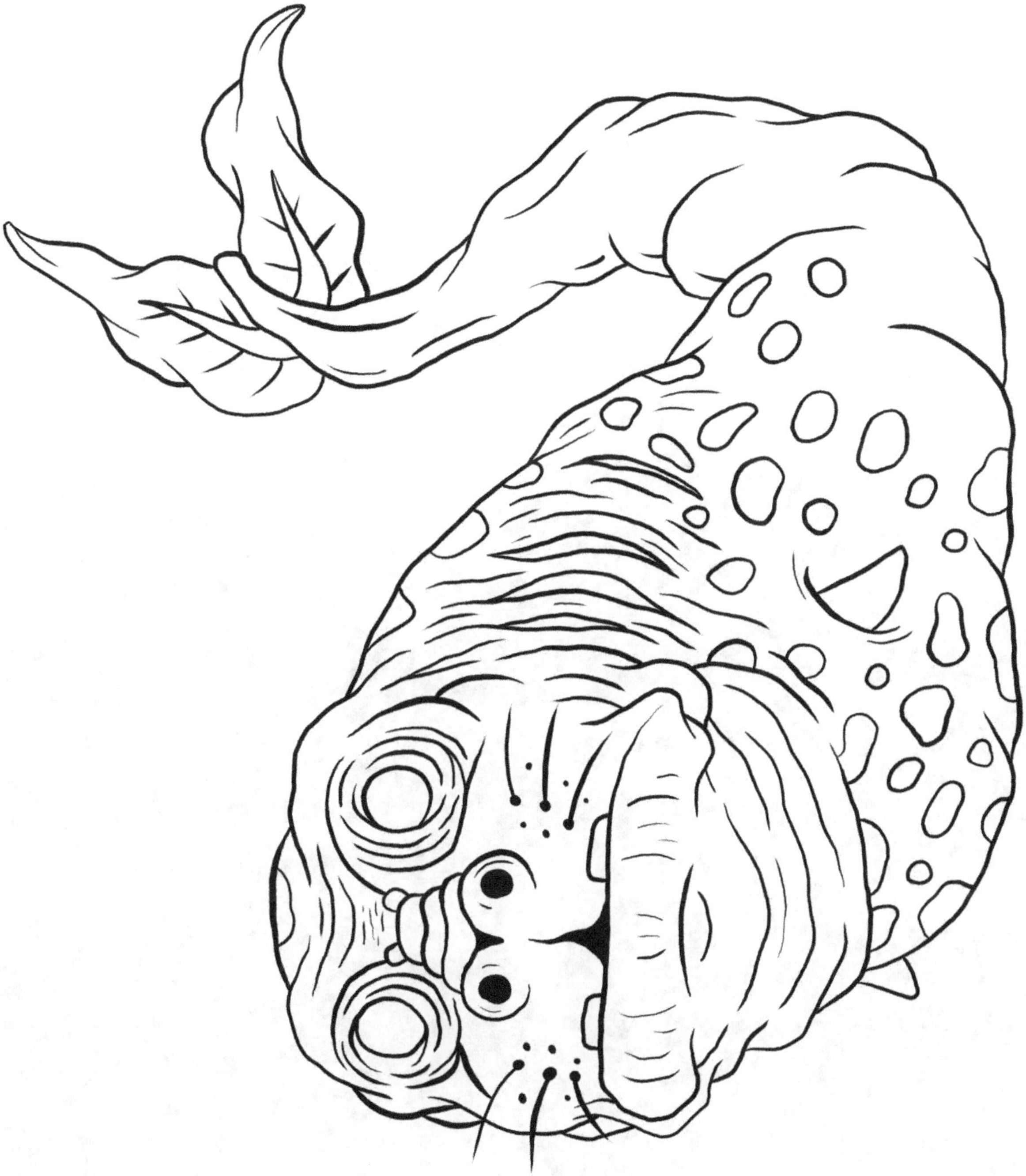

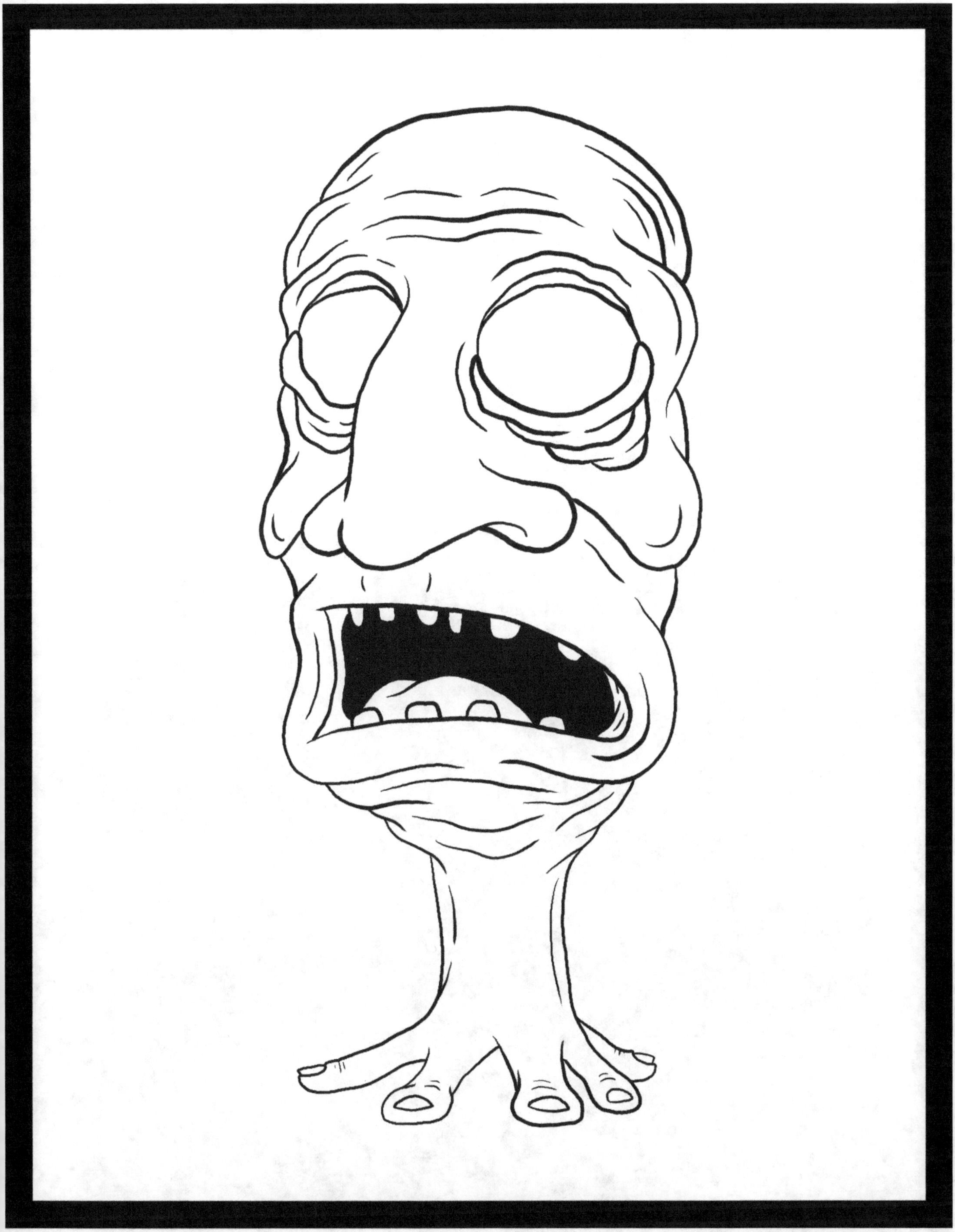

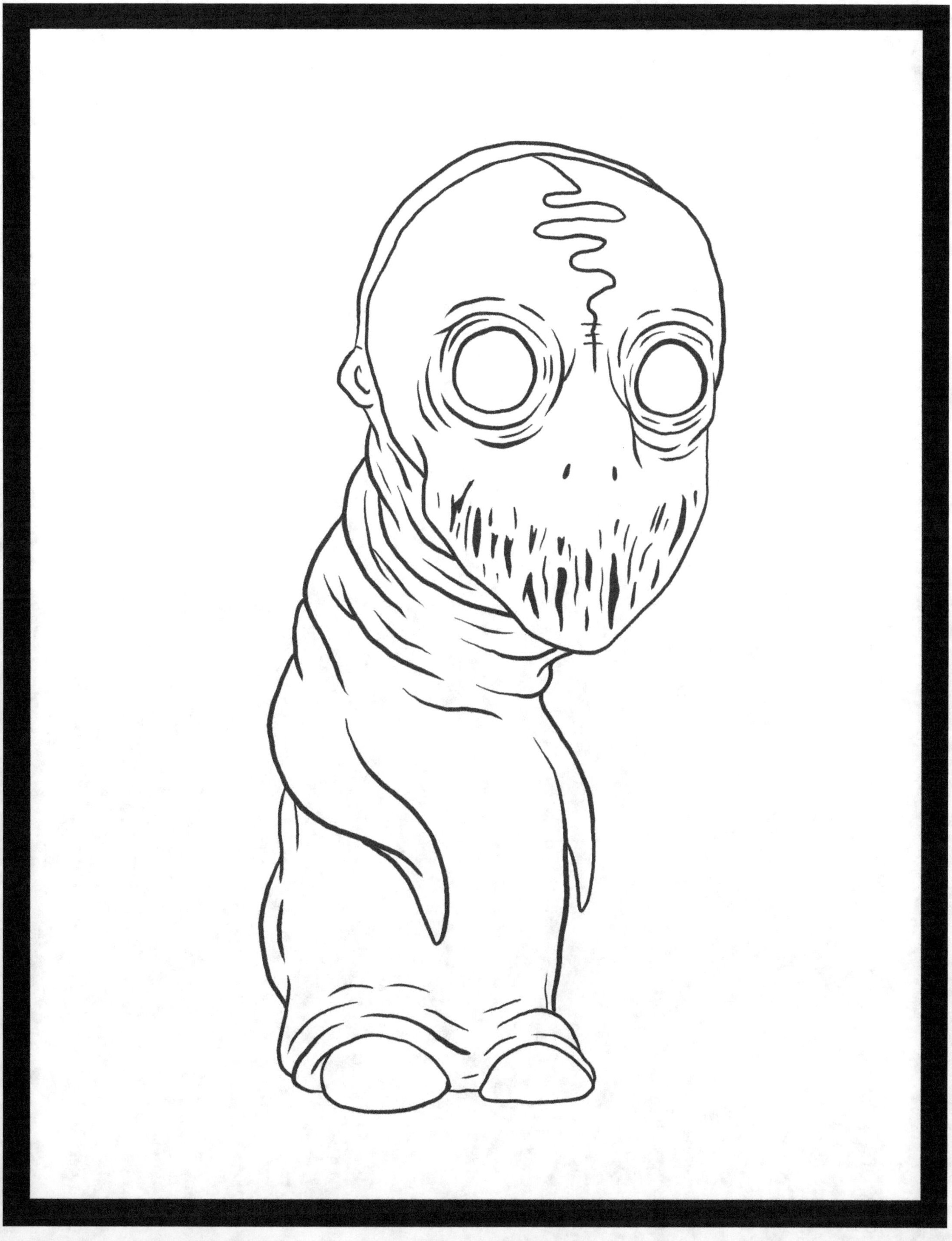

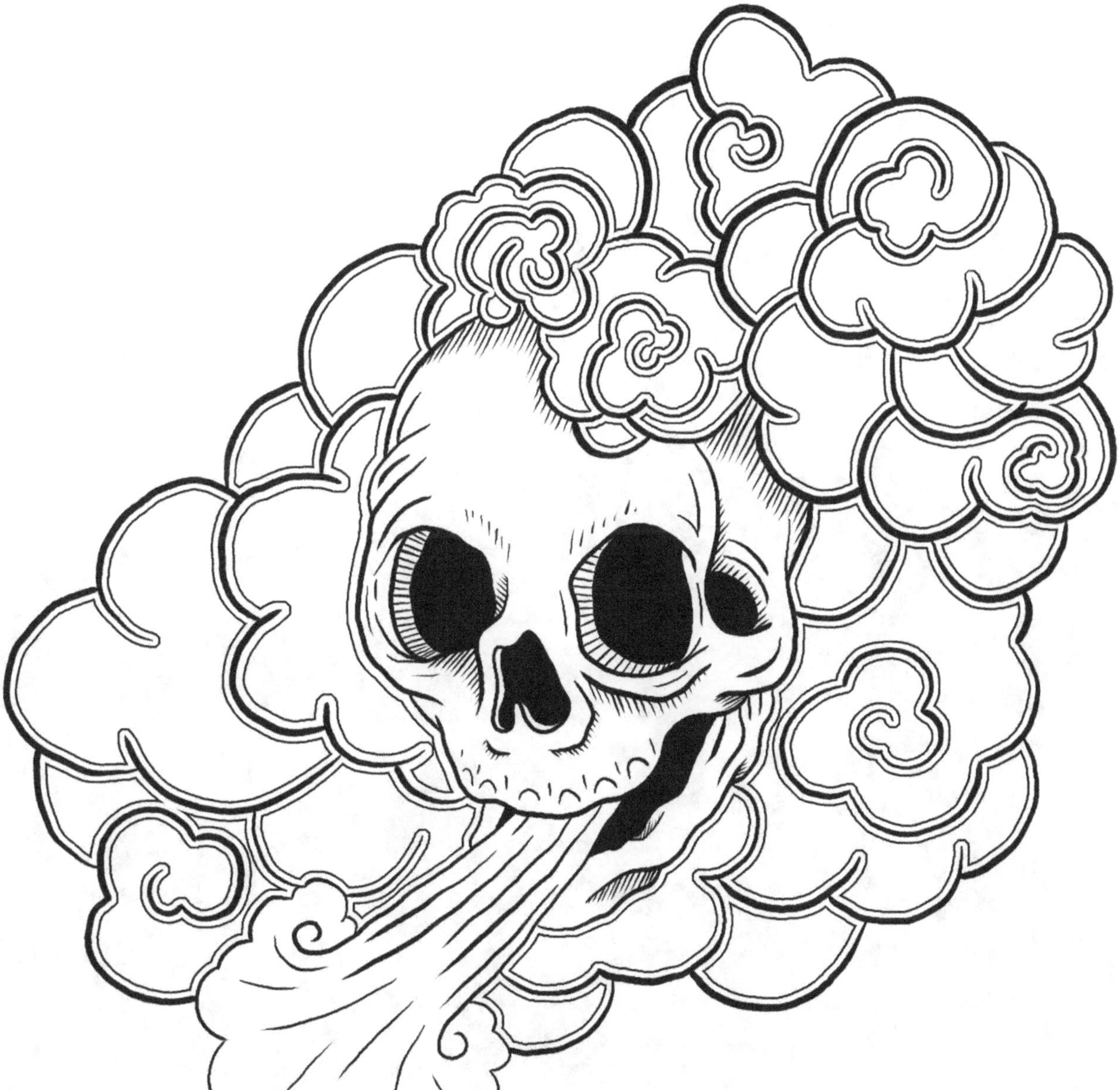

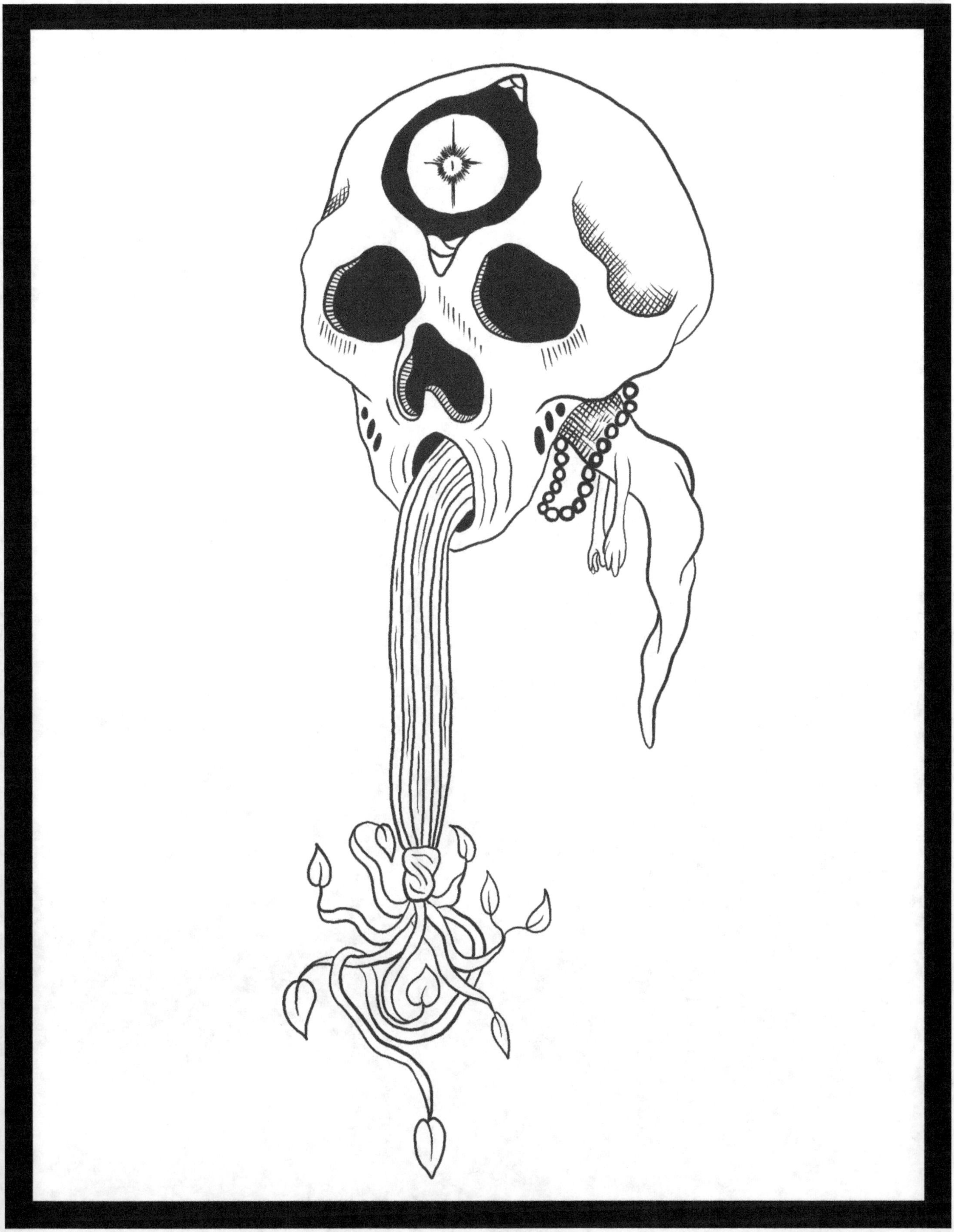

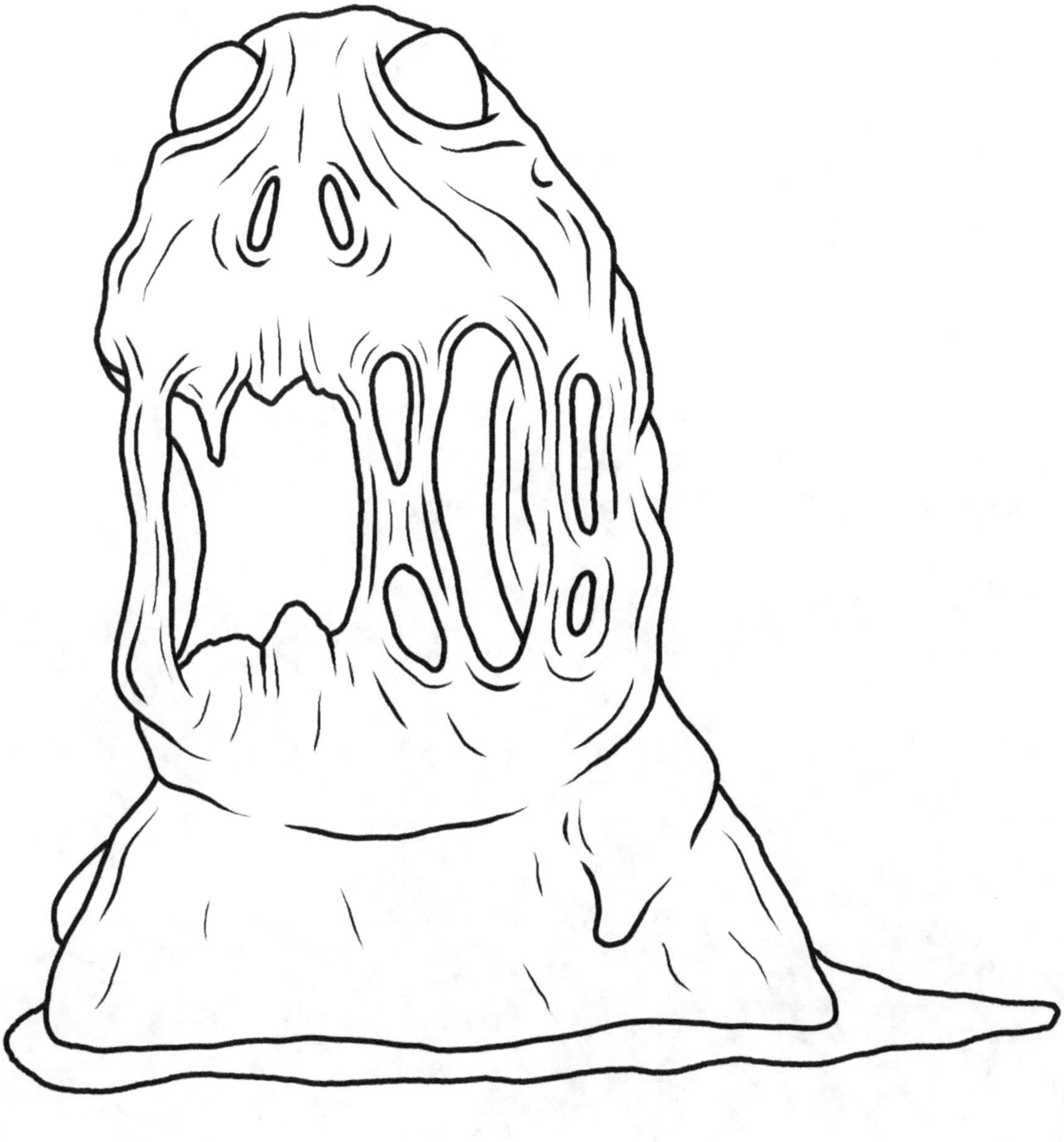

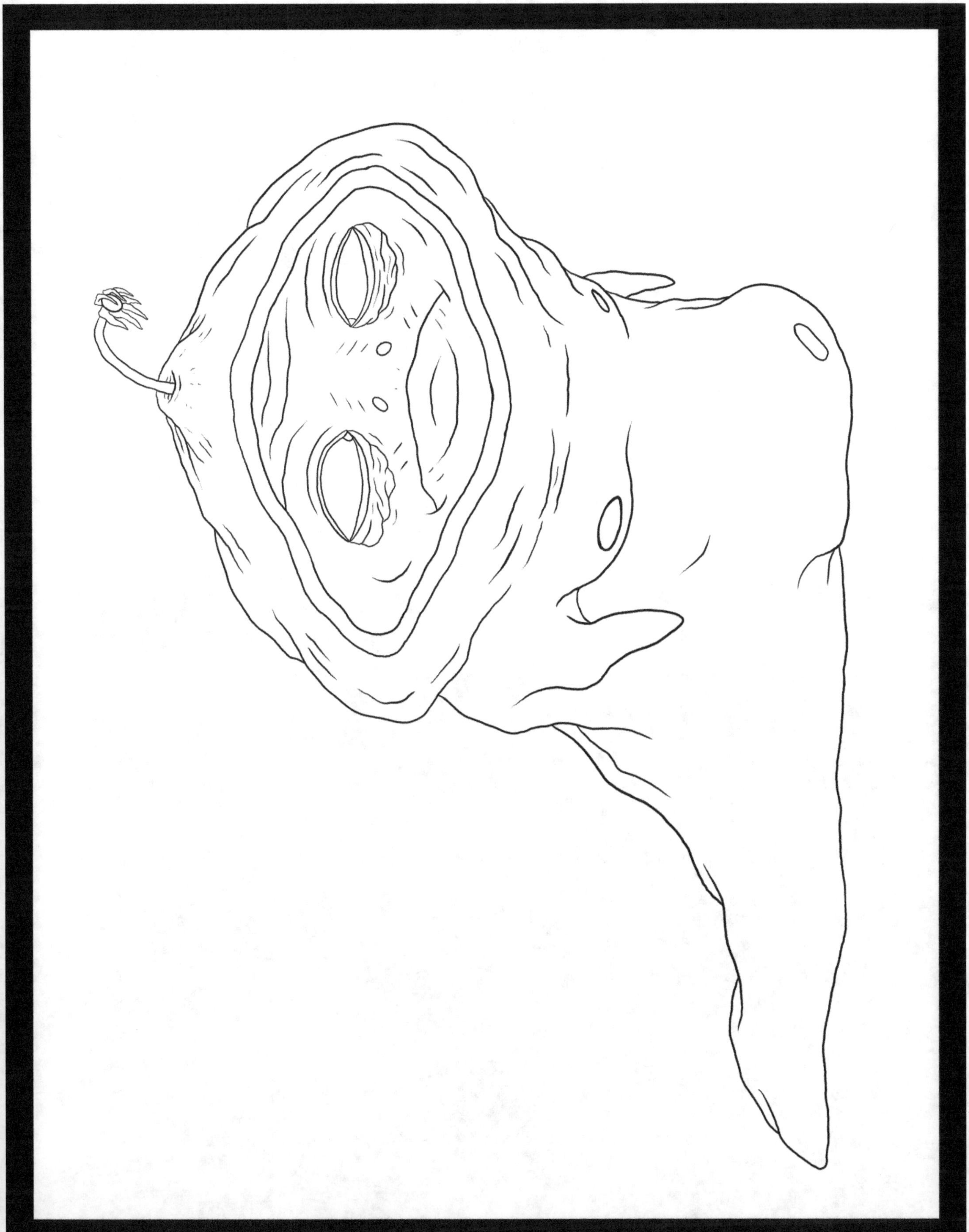

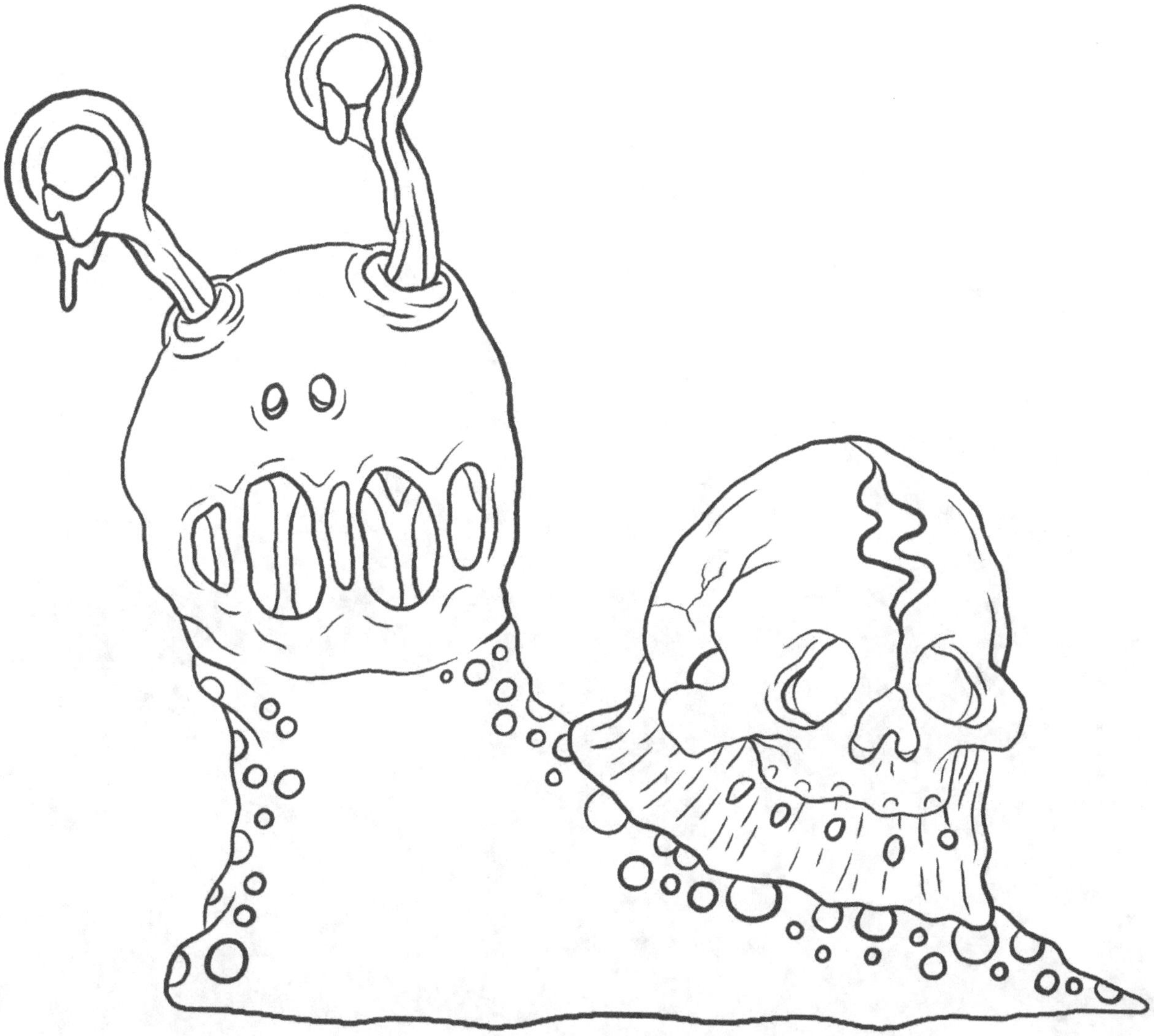

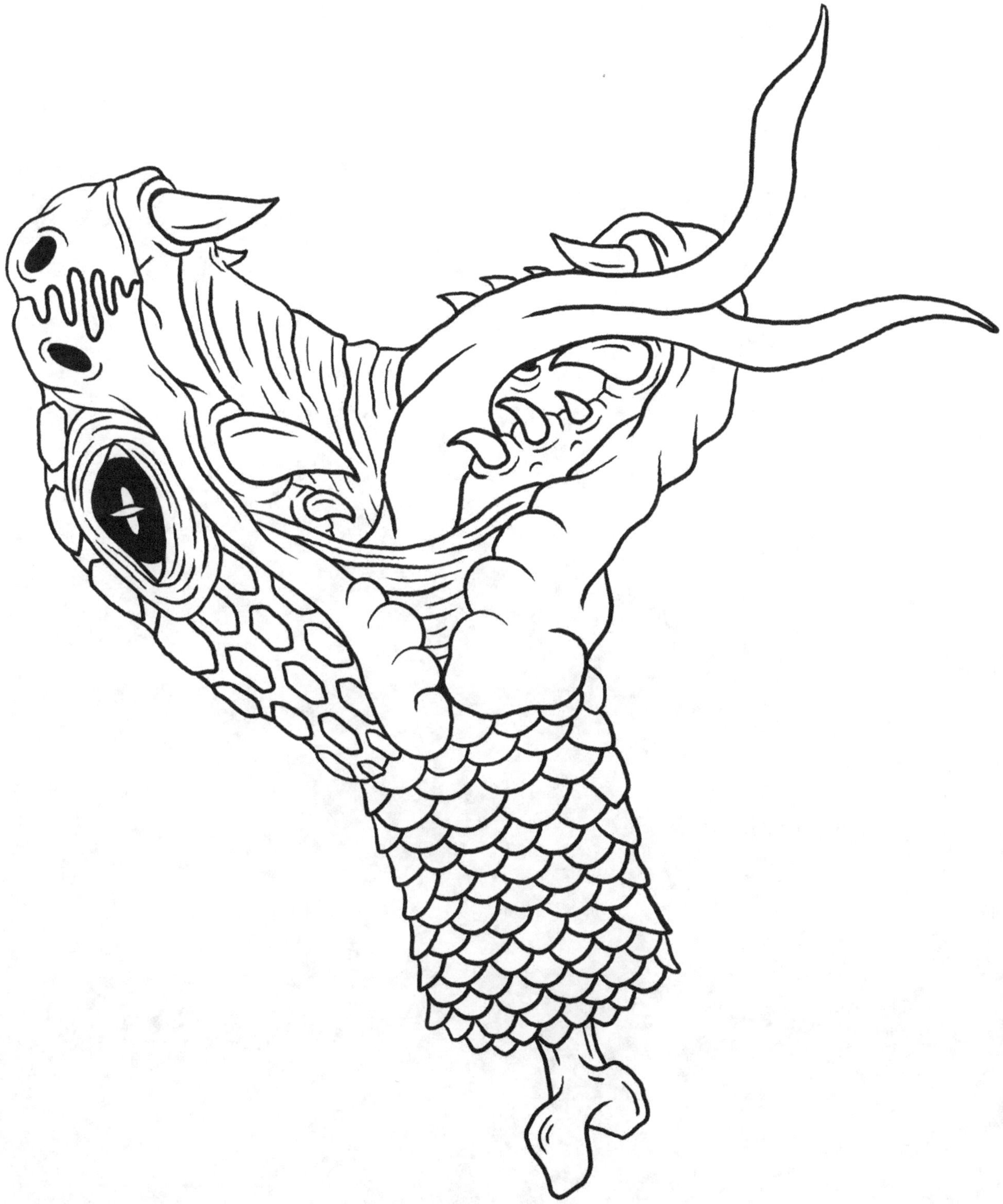

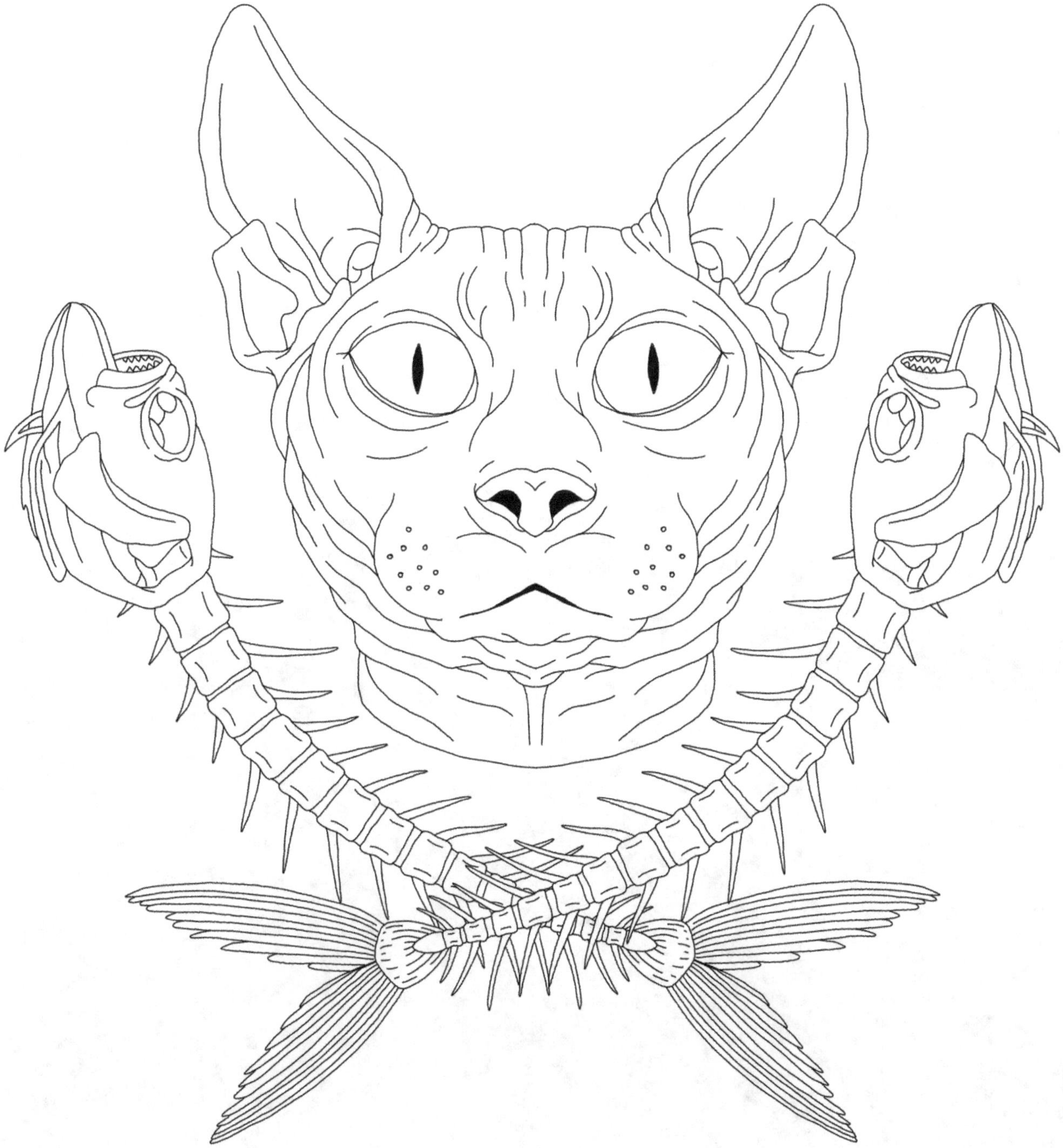

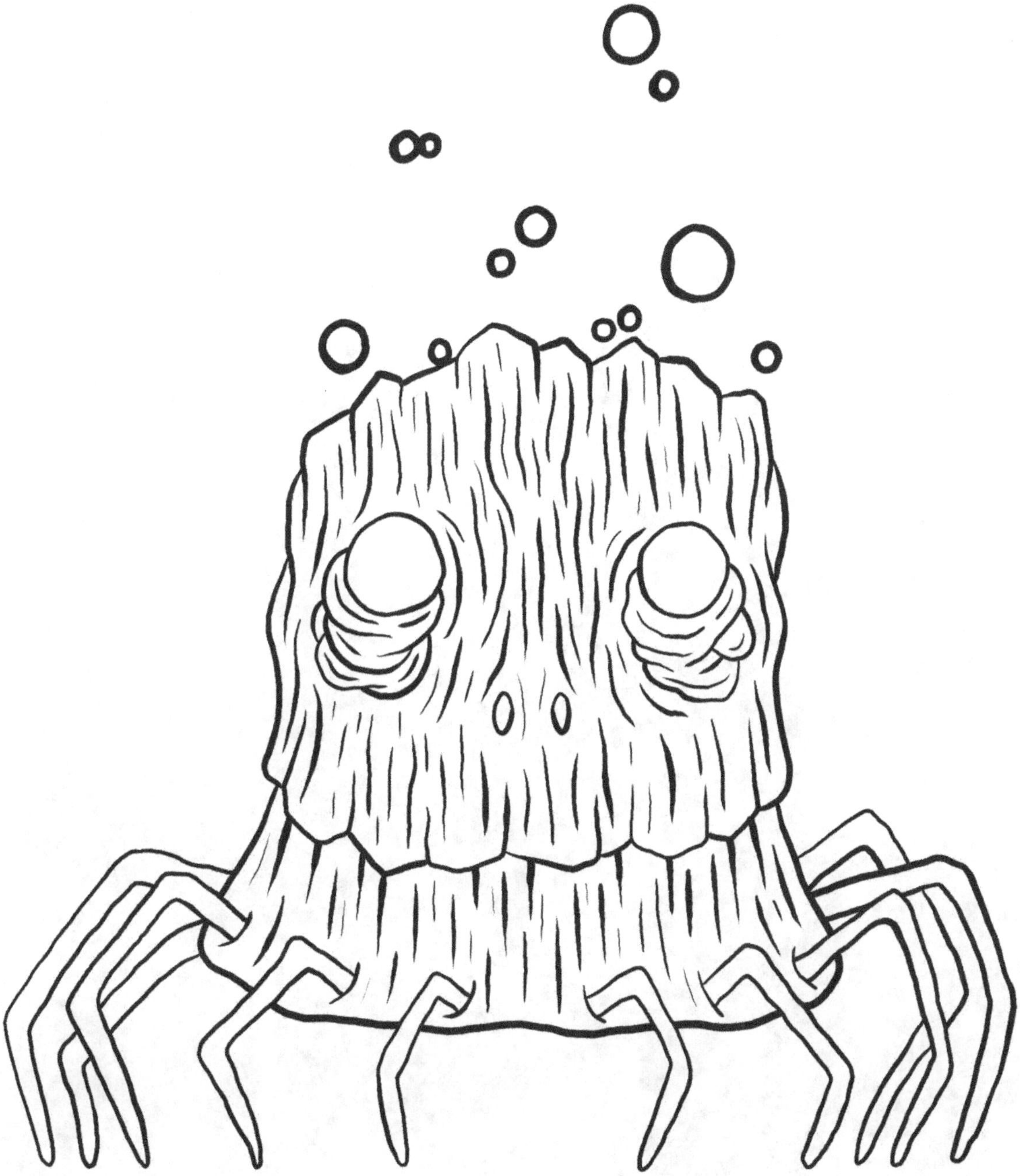

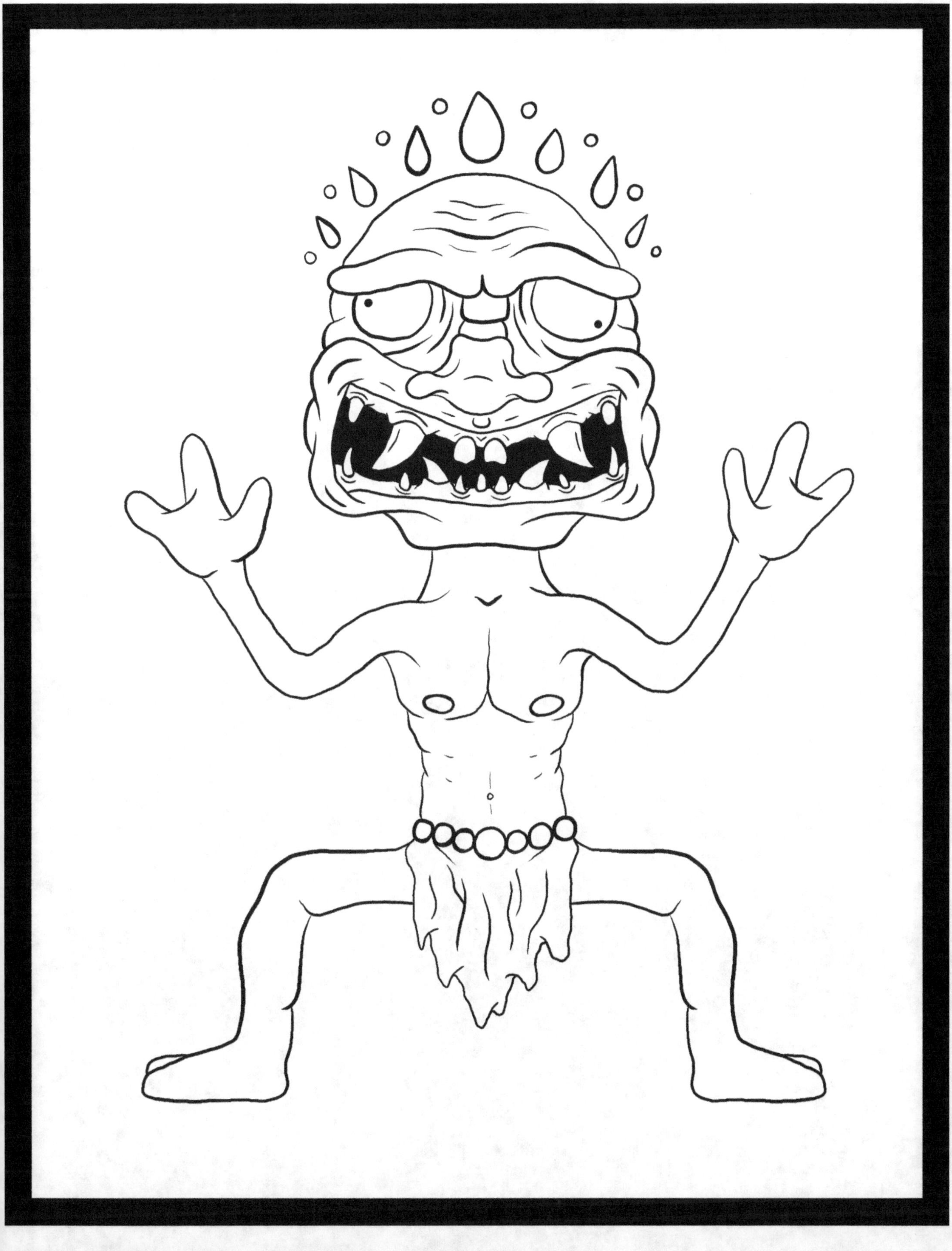

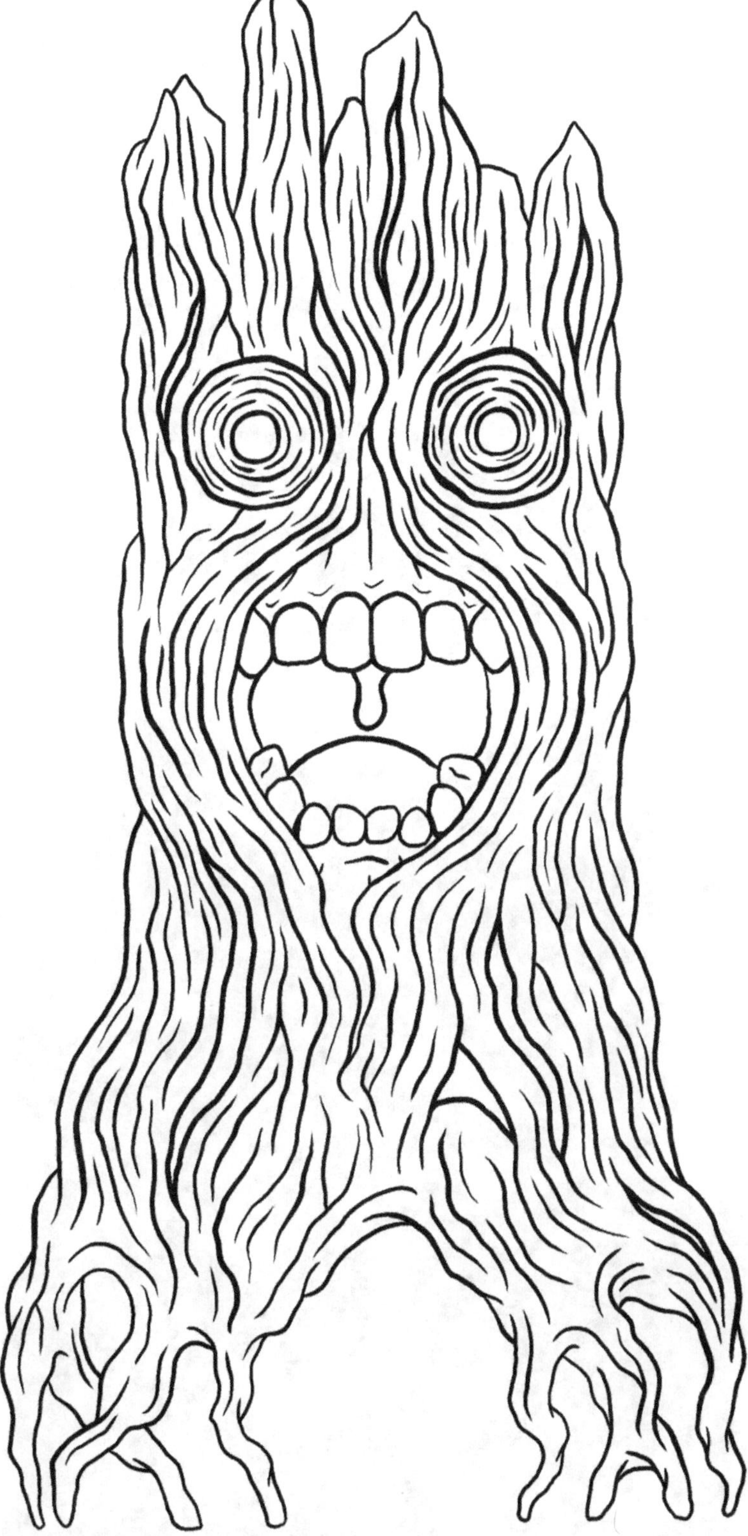

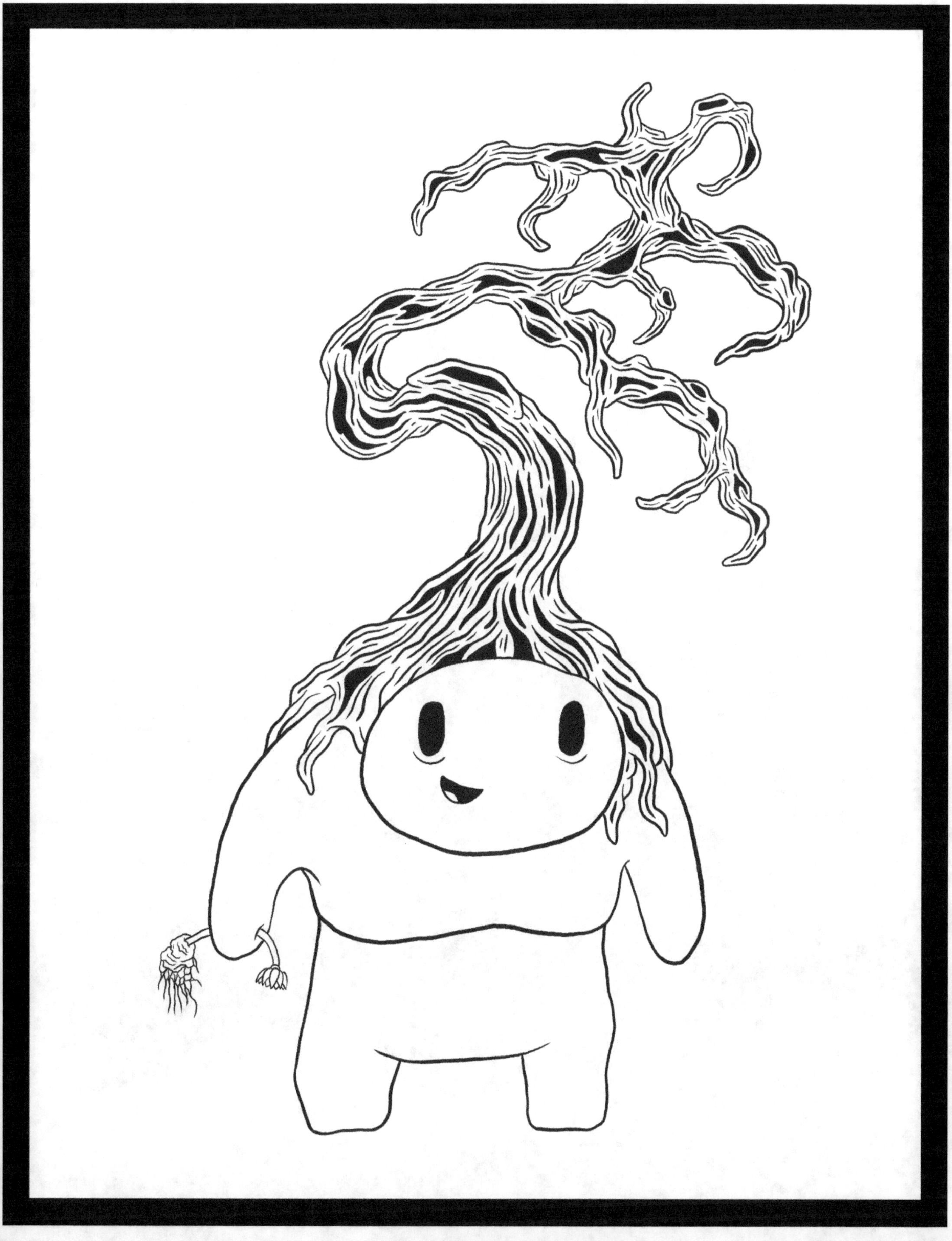

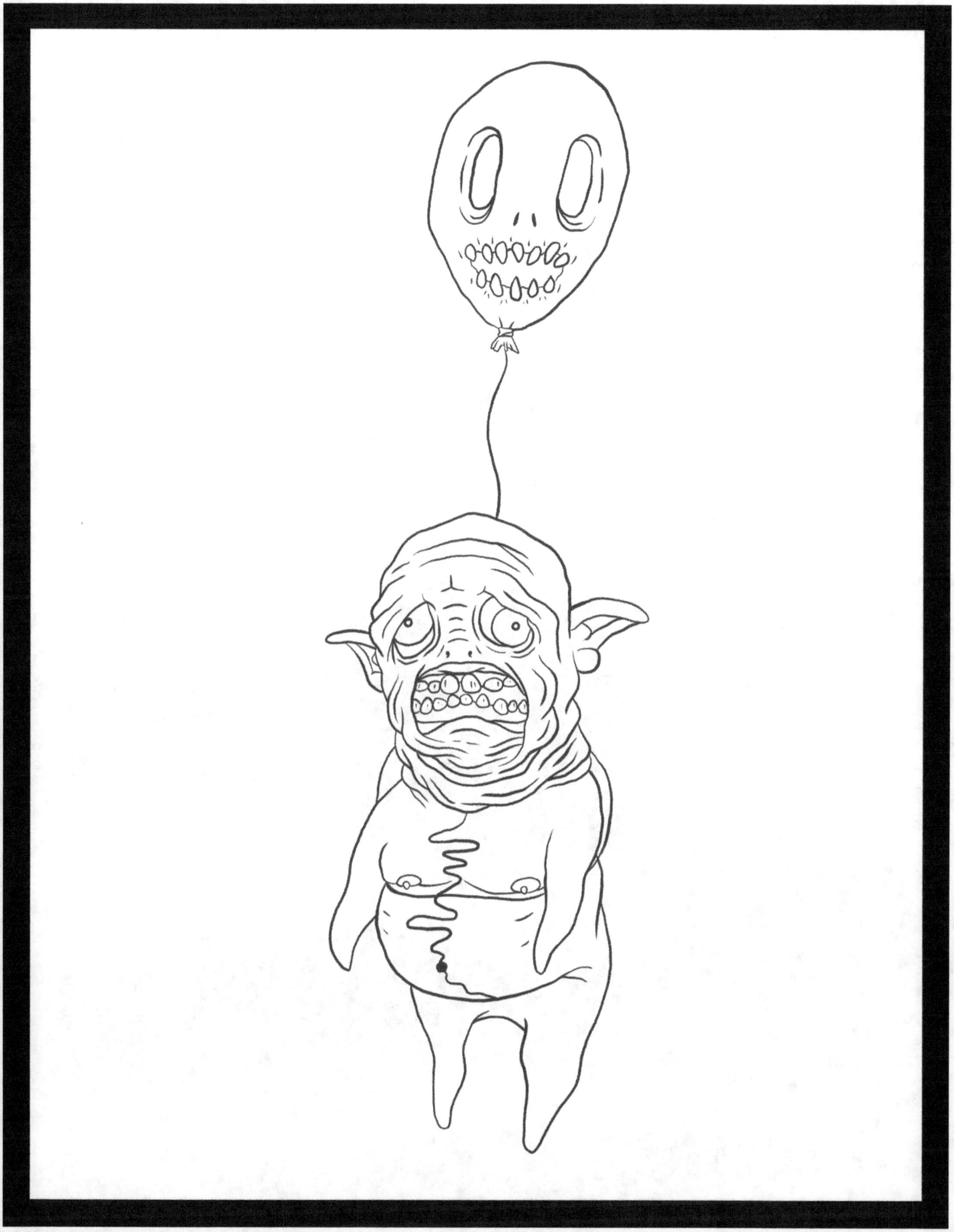

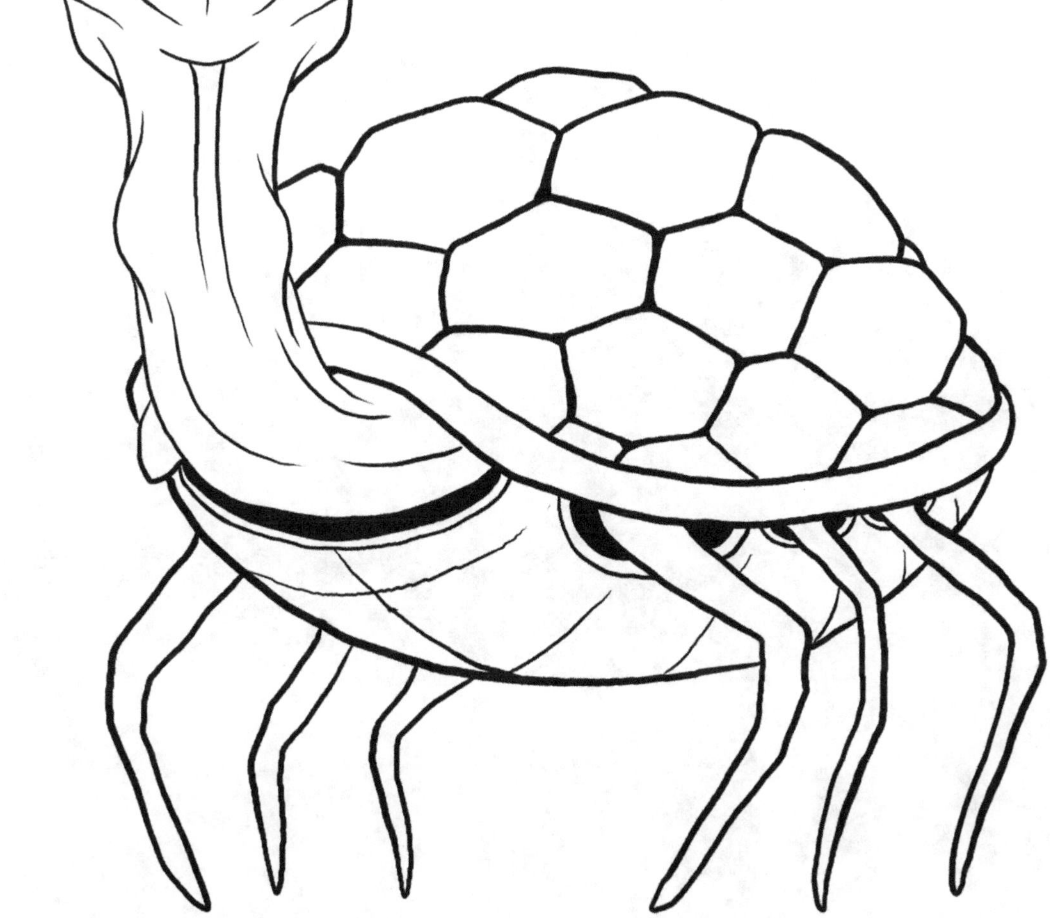

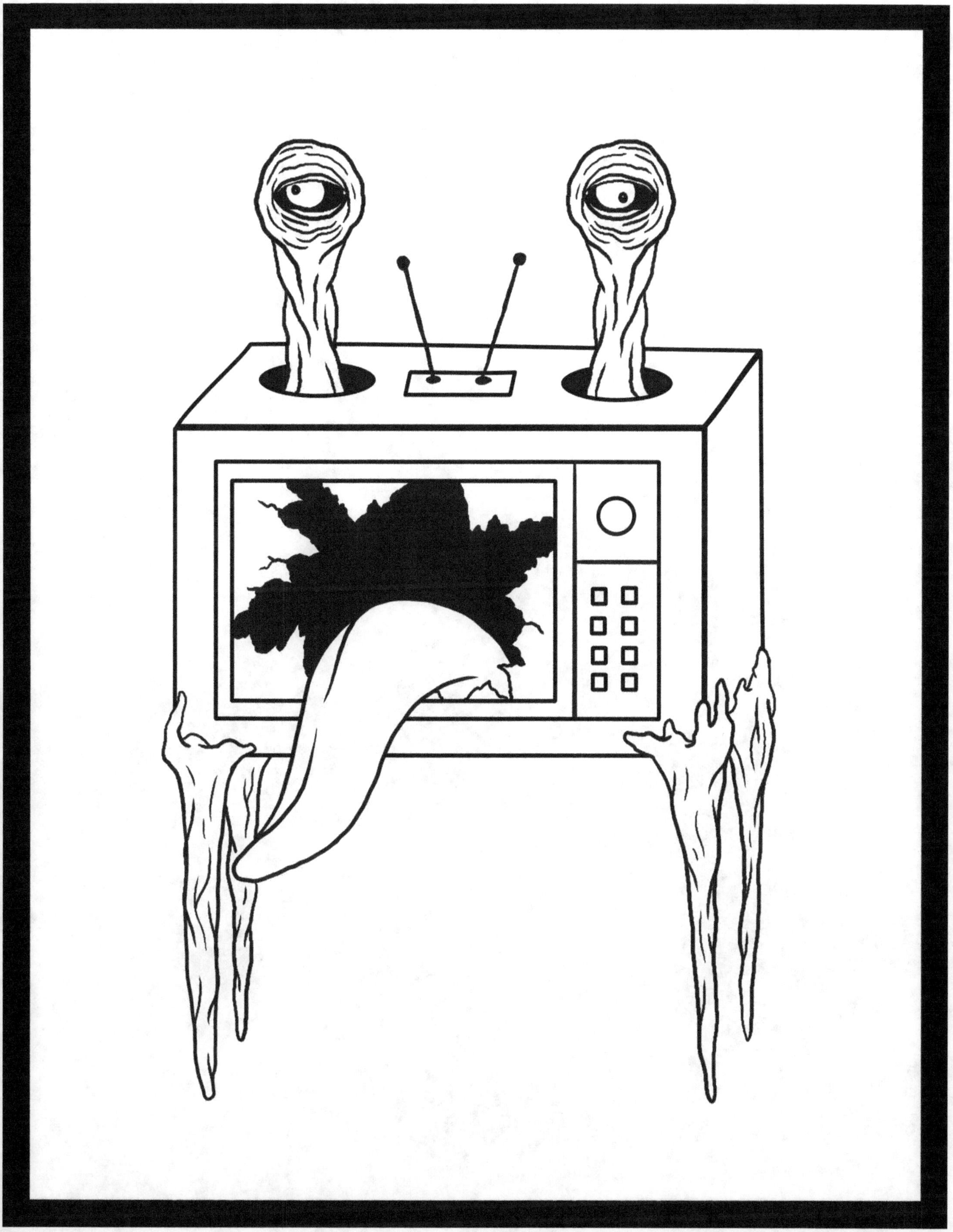

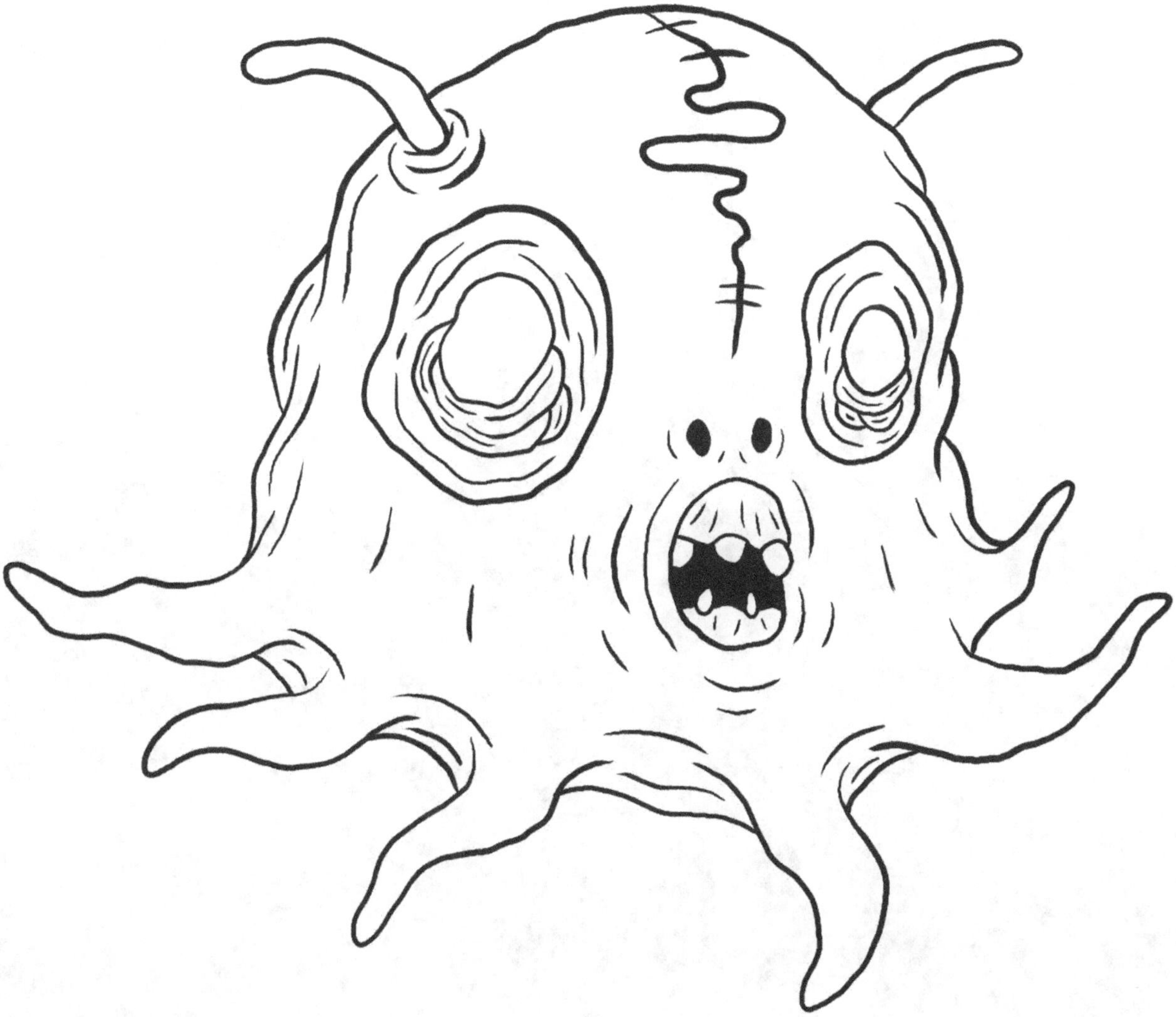

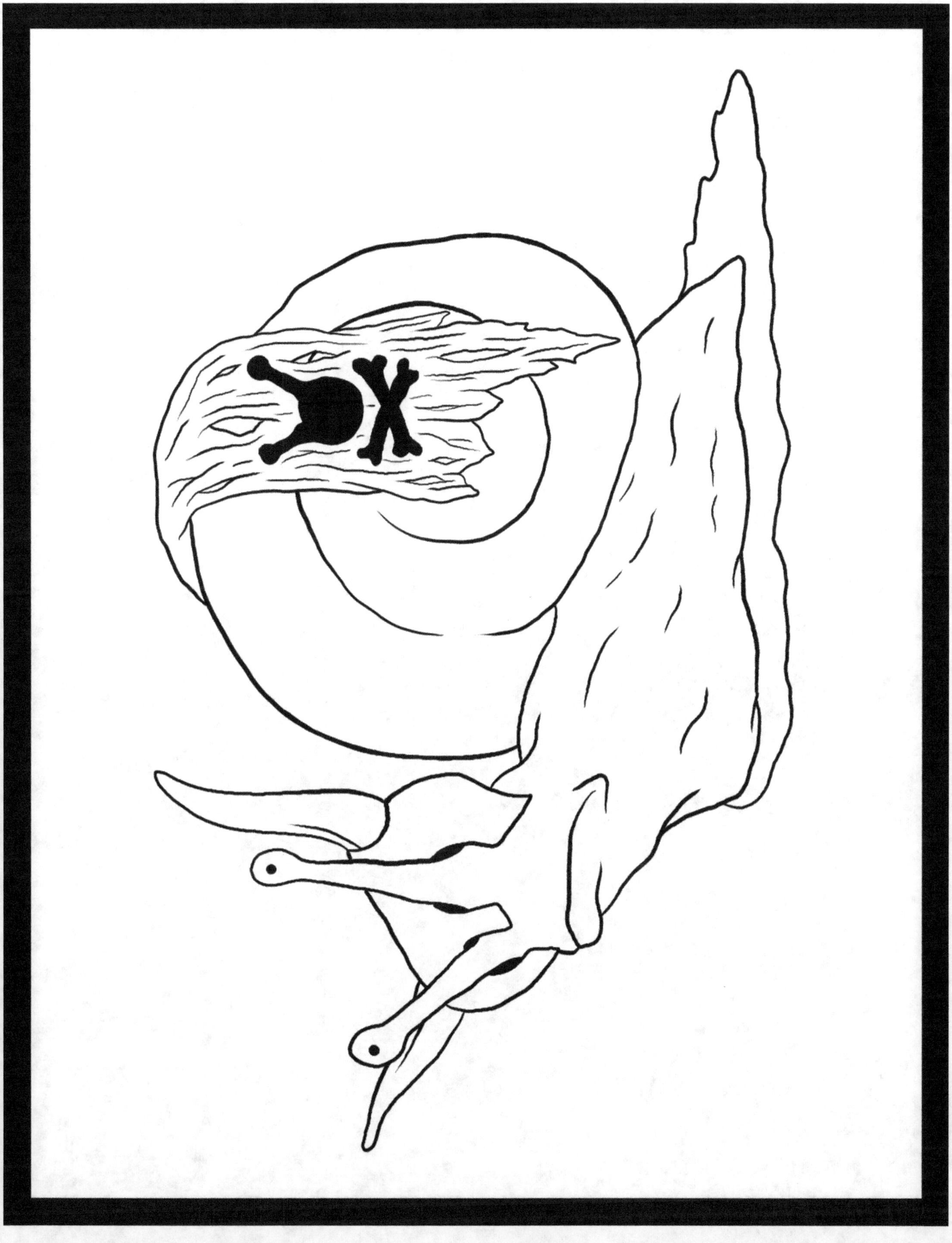

www.ingramcontent.com/pod-product-compliance
Lightning Source LLC
Chambersburg PA
CBHW080839220526
45467CB00008B/2333
* 9 7 9 8 6 8 6 2 6 6 8 4 1 *